Fringford
Through the Ages

Martin Greenwood

© 2000 Martin Greenwood
Published by Martin Greenwood.

ISBN 0-9539627-0-9

Design and artwork by
Brendan Rallison.

Printed in Great Britain by the
Alden Group, Oxford.

Front Cover:
The Forge c.1898 with William Plumb in the cart; the boys
may be Mrs Whitton's grandsons (Bill Plumb)

CONTENTS

Acknowledgements	2
Foreword	3
1. The Changing Village	5
2. A Stroll round the Village	13
3. Church and Clergy	39
4. Schools and Education	45
5. The Roll of Honour	53
6. Candleford Green Revisited	57

Maps

1. The Fringford area	4
2. Fringford c.1900	12
Appendix 1: Fringford Tithe Award 1848 with part of the Tithe Map of 1856	66
Appendix 2: Fringford Rectors 1103-2000	68
Appendix 3: Note from Winston Churchill to Jack Standen in 1945	69
Bibliography and detailed references	71
Contact details	72

Acknowledgements

I must first thank the members of the Parish Council, in particular Michael Barrett, for their assistance in obtaining a Millennium grant to cover the printing and publication costs of this booklet. Many local people have generously given help and information in the writing of the booklet. In particular, I would like to thank Gladys Hinks, who has lived in the village for over 80 years and has been a wonderful source of information and photographs. My thanks to Gordon and Margaret Allen (especially for some of the photographs taken by Gordon's father in the 1920s), Myrtle Ayris, Sue Gahan, Les Golder, Bill Grantham, Phil Green, Joan Hawes, Charles and Jinkie Hebditch, Judy Legg (née Standen), Stephanie Maciejewski, Clive Morgan, Norah Morgan, Bill Plumb (for his old photographs and information about the old forge), Vera Raby (née Judd), David Taylor and Margaret Wright. I am grateful to Baroness von Maltzahn for information on the Harrison family and for the use of several of her photographs. A special thank you to Elizabeth Bagley of Rexburg, Idaho and Pat Spence of Sandstone Point, Queensland for the photograph and letters of their ancestor, Sarah Butler Rennison. My thanks to the Oxford Archaeological Unit for use of their report on Farriers Close. Thanks also to Banbury County Museum for the use of a previously unpublished photograph of Flora Thompson. It is impossible to mention the names of all those I have spoken to or to tell all their tales in these pages.

I would like to thank Julie Barrett for her artistry in creating the maps. My thanks to Robert Treen for his computer wizardry in scanning the photographs, to Robert Young for project management and to Brendan Rallison for his significant design input. As a novice writer, I am particularly grateful to Rachel Howe of the Alden Press for all her help and encouragement. My thanks to the staff of the Westgate Centre for Oxfordshire Studies for their assistance with all my queries, to Debbie Vernon and Alec McNab for their proof-reading and constructive criticism and to my wife, Anne, for all her patience while I have been researching and writing this booklet.

Finally, a big thank you to the Millennium Awards for All Committee which has made a grant to cover the costs of producing the booklet. This will allow the proceeds to be shared between Fringford Church of England Primary School, St Michael and All Angels Church and the Village Hall.

Foreword

The Millennium has provided the impetus for the writing of this booklet on Fringford. I have been researching the village records for some years in connection with my local history studies. Millennium Year seemed a perfect time to make use of this research to produce a new booklet on the village. The Victoria County History of Fringford was printed as long ago as 1959 and the Revd John Sergeant's short guide in 1977.

The project started life as a simple guide in the form of a stroll round the village. I was encouraged by the possibility of a Millennium grant to involve the community, particularly the older residents before their memories of the village were lost. A questionnaire was sent to all the older houses in the village, asking the occupants for information, documents, photographs and stories about their houses and previous occupants. The excellent response has given me a wealth of information, old photographs and documents, for which I am very grateful. I have also spent many happy hours talking to the older residents about their memories of the village. If I have missed anyone, I must apologise. I am enormously grateful to all of you and I like to think that you too have enjoyed recalling the old times.

Wherever possible I have verified the accuracy of the information which I have received and the stories which I have been told. I have no doubt that there are still some inaccuracies. It is in the nature of local history to find conflicting evidence and some legends, well-founded or otherwise, where it is difficult to establish the original facts. I can only hope that there is both value and interest, and perhaps some entertainment, in what I have written, for past, present and future residents of the village.

In a small way, without Flora Thompson's unique gifts and insight, this has been an attempt in the year 2000 to look back at some of the changes since she lived in Candleford Green in the 1890s. Many of the stones and documents are still there to tell their stories. It is not always easy to read them or catch their 'whispers of history'. It has been a pleasure and a privilege to try and bring them to life, and to share the memories of those who have spent most of their life in the village.

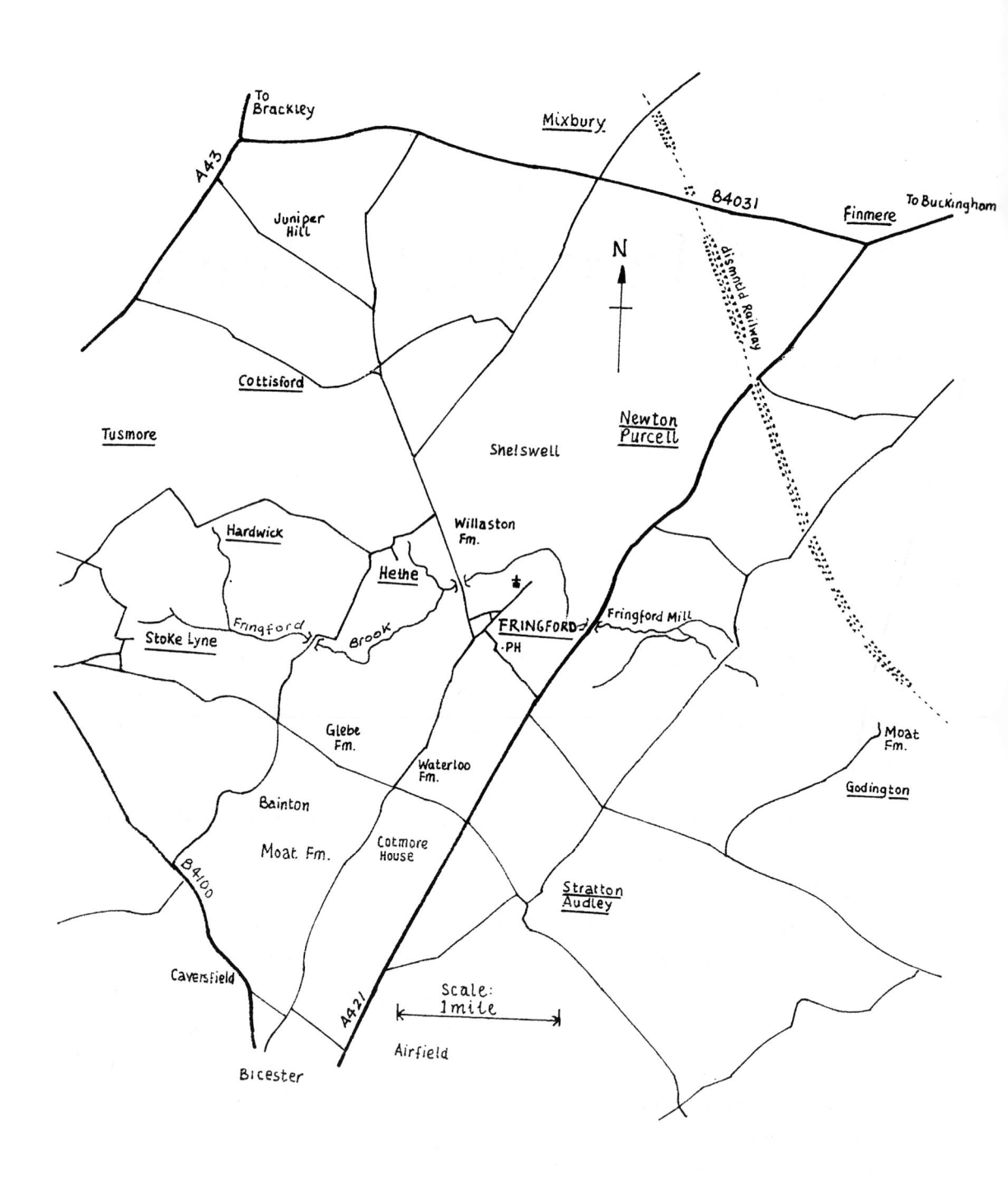

The Fringford area.
The ten parishes in the Shelswell Group are underlined.

Chapter 1

The Changing Village

The early years

Fringford is an ancient site and seems to have been inhabited for most, if not all, of the past 2000 years. The name is thought to mean "ford of the people of Fera", a Saxon tribe or family group, who were here well before the Norman Conquest. In 1993 traces of an earlier Romano-British settlement, from the late second century to the fourth century, were found in Crosslands in the centre of the village. Other work, at Fringford Lodge on the Bicester road, produced evidence of a possible Romano-British villa. More recent excavations in Farriers Close revealed a series of Iron Age and Romano-British boundary ditches overlain by Saxon and medieval settlements.[1]

The most unusual discovery was a Romano-British cremation burial with a large number of iron nails. It is likely that the individual had been wearing hobnailed boots and was placed in a wooden coffin before being burnt on a cremation pyre. There are no other known examples from Oxfordshire of such a cremation burial with footwear. In the second half of the thirteenth century, three stone buildings were constructed, one of which appears to have been a farrier's workshop. The buildings may have formed part of a manorial complex before they were apparently abandoned during the fourteenth century. This was the period of the Black Death and other plagues, which led to large-scale depopulation and the disappearance of villages like Tusmore. Significant medieval remains have also been found at Fringford Manor, including evidence of a medieval moated site and fish pond.

Fringford lies in a loop of the River Ouse, with Fringford Bridge on the north-west and the old cornmill and Fringford Mill Bridge to the east. Blomfield noted traces of a ford in the late nineteenth century and said that once a road (now Rectory

Lane) ran from the village green west of the Rectory down to the stream and that a stone paved way went to Willaston. He also made the credible suggestion that there was a second ford on the site of Fringford Bridge, which was used after the hamlet of Shelswell became depopulated in the sixteenth century and its traffic diverted to Hethe and Cottisford.[2] Sheep pasture became more economic than arable land and so 'sheep ate up men'. The Lord of Shelswell Manor evicted 11 people, enclosed the fields and converted them to pasture. By 1601 the enclosure of Shelswell was complete and the last of the village disappeared soon afterwards. Towards the middle of the nineteenth century the present Fringford Bridge replaced a narrow single-arch bridge, of which some traces remain.

Enclosure and the major landowners

In the seventeenth century, the Hearth Tax returns of 1665 and the Compton Census of 1676 indicate that there were some 30 houses in Fringford and a population of about 130. During the eighteenth century, the village grew and by 1801 there were about 50 houses and a population of 252. By the time of the Enclosure Award in 1762, some 400 to 500 acres had already been enclosed by agreement, most of it for the manor owned by Sir Fulke Greville. The Award effectively meant the end of the open field system with its medieval style of farming in strips. Under the Award, Greville received 385 acres, while the other principal beneficiaries were the rector, the Revd John Russell Greenhill (227 acres), Anthony Addington of Hall Farm (89 acres) and Eton College (71 acres). Eton College also owned most of the neighbouring parish of Cottisford.

In the sixteenth century, there were still two manors in Fringford, the North Manor on the site of the Old School, occupied by the Wenmans, and the South Manor probably on the site of Moat Farm (formerly Cotmore Farm). By 1762, both the manor houses had disappeared. Shortly after enclosure, the North Manor's lands were sold to Lord Holland, who in turn sold them in 1815 to John Harrison. Harrison's father had bought the neighbouring Shelswell Manor, which with its large estate dominates the surrounding area. In 1844, it was reported that 'Nearly if not the whole of Fringford is the property of JHS Harrison Esq'.[3] (The Tithe Award of 1848 does show that he owned 50 of the 83 properties listed (see Appendix 1). Under the Award, tithes (a tenth part of a person's income paid to the rector in cash or kind) were commuted to a rent-charge. In 1875, the old manor was pulled down and a new one built in its place. The Harrisons and the Slater-Harrisons continued to live here until the manor was abandoned and finally pulled down in the early 1980s. In 1967, on the death of John Dewar-Harrison, often referred to as 'the last squire', his goddaughter, Baroness von Maltzahn, succeeded him as Lord of the Manor.

Edward Slater-Harrison in 1902 shooting near Newton Morrell (Baroness von Maltzahn)

John Dewar-Harrison (mounted) talking to Lord Chesham at a Meet of the Bicester Hounds at Fringford Bridge in 1923/24 (Baroness von Maltzahn)

The Addington family have also retained their local connection. They still own Hall Farm, although Anthony Addington left in the eighteenth century to become a fashionable London doctor and included George III among his patients. His son, Henry, became Speaker of the House of Commons, Prime Minister and the first Lord Sidmouth. John Russell Greenhill was rector of Fringford (1756-1813) for nearly 60 years, and for the following 80 years Fringford enjoyed the reigns of three 'regal' rectors: Henry Roundell (1814-52), Henry Fane de Salis (1852-73) and Cadwallader Coker (1873-94). All these rectors were well-connected, wealthy men, who were prepared to make substantial contributions to the church and parish (see Chapter 3). Eton College, the other major landowner, sold off its remaining holdings in Cottisford and Fringford in 1921-22. The College's main holdings in Fringford were around the Mill and Church Farm (see Appendix 1).

The nineteenth century

Fringford in the nineteenth century is now forever associated with Flora Thompson's *Lark Rise to Candleford*. In it she recalls her childhood, as Flora Timms *(Laura)*, in the hamlet of Juniper Hill *(Lark Rise)* and at school in Cottisford *(Fordlow)* before moving to Fringford *(Candleford Green)*. It is a unique and vivid picture of village life at the end of the nineteenth century. There is hardly a page without a memorable phrase waiting to be quoted. She largely bases *Candleford Green* on her childhood memories of Fringford, when she worked in the village post office from 1891 to 1897. In many respects, village life had changed very little in the decades before 1876, when she was born. Deference to those above you was the norm and 'Every member of the community knew his or her place and few wished to change it'![4] It was a defining moment just before the agricultural depression of the 1870s and 1880s and before the impact of major changes in health, housing and education.

Fringford Population 1801-1991

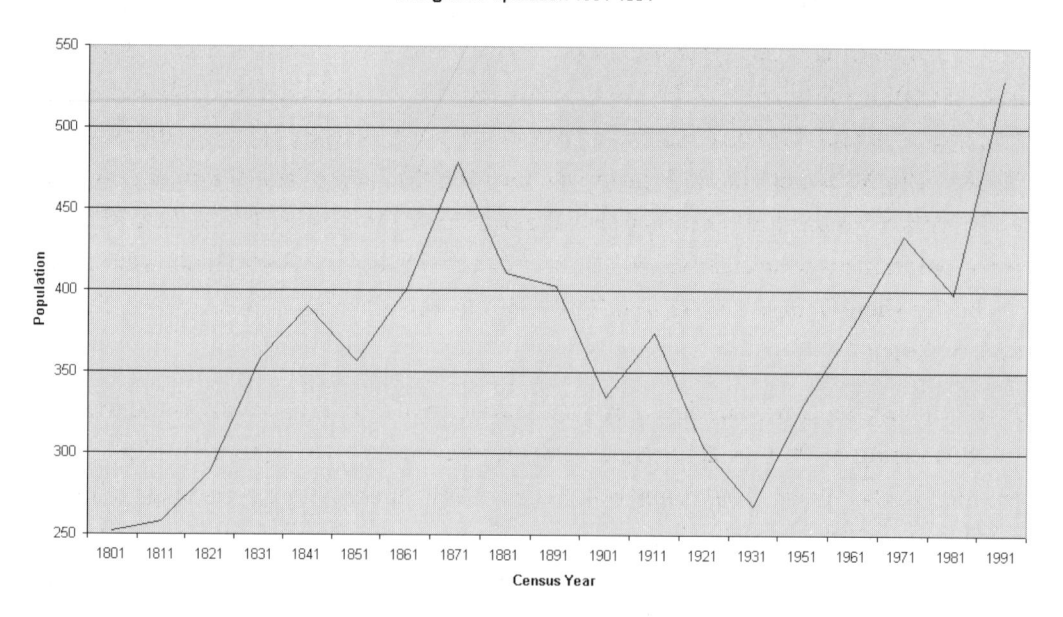

In 1844, there had not been 'dwellings enough to shelter the poor' in Fringford.[5] In 1851, when the population was 357, the 76 houses in the parish were generally modest with only a few good farm-houses to impress the visitor. There was relative prosperity until 1871, when the population reached its peak of 479. The last quarter of the century saw a decline and in the 1890s a second agricultural depression brought a general exodus from the country to the towns. It also led many to emigrate to Australia, Canada and the United States. Emma Dibber, Flora Thompson's mother, nearly joined some of her relatives in Australia before she was married. Although she decided against it, Frank, one of her sons, and Basil, one of Flora's sons, both emigrated to Australia. The numbers emigrating from the United Kingdom were very large, some six million between 1871 and 1911, most of them to the United States, Canada and Australia.[6] As a result, there was a general decline in village populations and rural trades. By 1901 there were 94 houses in the parish but the population had dropped sharply from 403 in 1891 to 335, its lowest point since the 1820s.

People in *Candleford Green* are shown generally as poor and largely dependent on agricultural occupations. Their lives are simple but hard, with few luxuries. Census returns confirm how dependent Fringford, like other parishes in the area, was on agricultural occupations. There were 61 labourers living in the parish in 1851 and a similar number in 1891, when the youngest recorded labourer was only eleven. There would have been others, perhaps as young as eight, also working on the farms and not spending much time in school. There were seven active farms in 1851, all of them labour-intensive. John King at Waterloo Farm was farming 515 acres with 23 labourers and Thomas Simons at Manor Farm 276 acres with 11 labourers. In 1861, John Mansfield at Hall Farm was farming 200 acres with 9 men and 4 boys and George Gibbard at The Laurels 50 acres with 3 men and 1 boy. In 1891, the principal farmers were still Henry King at Waterloo Farm and John Simons at Manor Farm. By then George Gibbard at The Laurels was described as a brewer, farmer and maltster.

If you include all those employed in occupations related to agriculture, there were 71 in 1851 rising to 90 in 1891. These totals represent 48% rising to 57% of all males over ten in the village. Trades and other occupations increase the percentage of males employed to 69% and 86%. Given the agricultural depression in the 1870s and 1880s, these figures seem very high and it is possible that some of the labourers may not have been so fully employed by 1891. Certainly, by 1901, after the second agricultural depression, the numbers and percentage employed would have been lower.

The wide range of trades in 1891 included five blacksmiths (including John Whitton, the Postmaster), three carpenters, three sawyers, three brickmakers, a stonemason, a cordwainer (shoemaker), three painter/decorators, a carrier, a coal haulier, two bakers, two grocers and a butcher. Other male occupations included two grooms, two footmen, six gardeners and a coachman, no doubt employed at Shelswell or another of the 'big houses'. On the female side, there was a large increase from nine to eighteen domestic and farm servants by 1891. There was a servant boom between 1851 and the end of the century, which saw numbers rise nationally from 750,000 to about 1.3 million. In the local area, Shelswell, Tusmore and Swift's House were major employers of servants and other staff.

The twentieth century

During the first half of the twentieth century, the major changes in health, housing and education were slow to reach rural villages like Fringford and daily life changed very little. By 1951, the population was still only 331 and most families remained largely dependent on agriculture. Electricity was not in general use until after the Second World War, mains water did not reach the village until about 1960 and the standard of housing after the War was still very basic. Daily life remained simple and hard with few luxuries and the village continued to be a largely self-sufficient community with its own shops, craftsmen and tradesmen. It also remained close-knit, judging by the number of intermarriages involving local names like Allen, Golder, Grantham, Hinks, Judd, Mansfield and Price.

It was not until after the Second World War that housing improved, with the building of 34 council houses on the Green and Stratton Audley Road. By then many of the older properties were in a very poor state of repair and some beyond repair. There was little money about and the days of barn and other conversions were many years ahead. The first housing developments came in the late 1960s in Church Close and St Michael's Close. In the 1980s new houses were built in The Laurels and Manor Road, when the farms were sold for development. In the 1990s, the last green spaces in the centre of the village disappeared, with the developments in Crosslands and Farriers Close. All this development has led to an influx of new residents, and the population has nearly doubled since 1951 to an estimated 600.

Today, the dependence on agriculture has largely disappeared and the only large-scale active farmer in the parish is David Taylor at Waterloo Farm. In sharp contrast to his father and grandfather, he farms some 1800 acres with just two helpers and some very large machinery. Alfred Taylor bought Glebe Farm in 1918 at the end of the First World War. His son, Henry, continued to farm there until he moved to Waterloo Farm in 1968, after John Dewar-Harrison left some of his farms to the tenants. By then the farmhouse, like many other buildings in the area, was very dilapidated and required some major renovations.

Waterloo Farm, and most of the older buildings in the parish, have now been modernised and the village has been transformed by all the new housing. It is easy to criticise some of the planning decisions and the variety of materials and styles which have been employed. The village may not be as attractive to some eyes but, in many respects, it is smarter and more prosperous than it has ever been. It is now over a hundred years since Flora Thompson worked in *Candleford Green* and so much has been altered and modernised. However, as we shall see in the following chapters, a surprising amount remains in the parish to interest her fans.

Fringford c. 1900

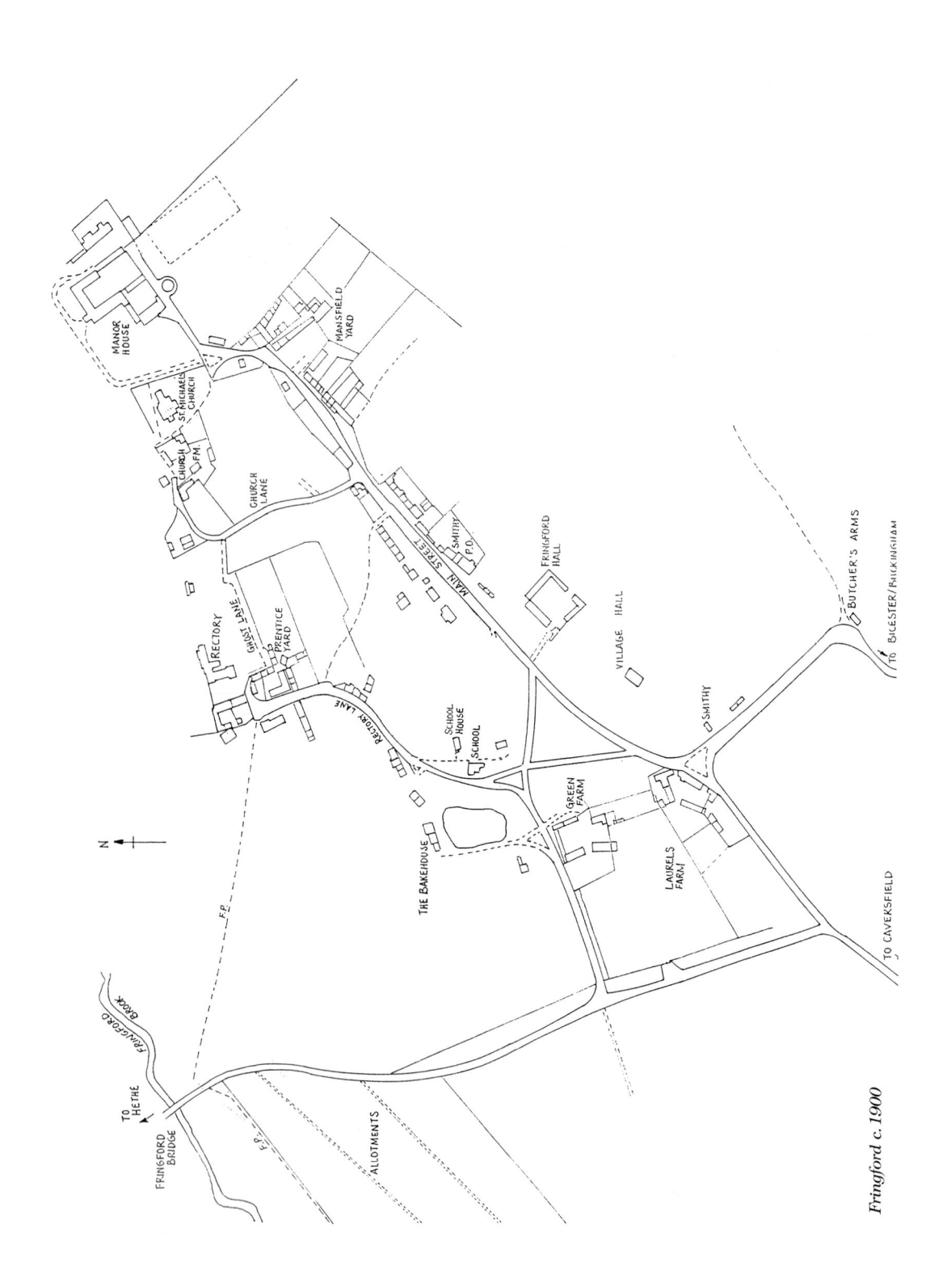

Chapter 2

A Stroll round the Village

This chapter invites you to take a stroll round the village, noting various items of interest along the way. The emphasis is on the older properties and the village as it was before the new housing developments, which started in the mid-1960s (see map).

We begin our walk on the Green outside the Village Hall and the Church of England Primary School.

The classic setting of the medieval village grouped round the GREEN survives. The old farmhouses here, Green Farm, Laurels Farm and Hall Farm, all date from well before the Enclosure Award of 1762. The farms outside the village, for example Waterloo Farm and Glebe Farm, were built after Enclosure. Waterloo Farm, on the back road to Caversfield, was built by Squire Harrison in 1815 soon after his purchase of the Shelswell Estate, and he 'named it after the great victory, which was at that time the talk of every tongue.'[7]

The VILLAGE HALL was built by Henry Chinnery in 1900 on land given by the squire of the parish, Mr Edward Slater-Harrison. It was formally opened in June 1900 by Mr Chinnery and presented to the village as a reading room for the men of the village and a place for meetings and entertainments. In 1901, it was described in the local press as 'the new parish room', where there was tea and entertainment on New Year's Day. The entertainment included singing, recitations and a cinematograph exhibition by Mr Timms of Oxford.[8] The kitchens were added in the early 1970s. The hall has been recently refurbished with Lottery money.

RINGFORD

The Laurels with the old smithy and cottage in the 1950s (Judy Legg)

The old smithy before conversion 1980s (Sue C

Mrs Omar's shop on t with the Butcher's Arms at the end 1950s Note her Morris 8 and the s Eldorado ice cream.(Sue C

Mrs Omar in her Ford Popular in the 1950s (Judy Legg)

The Stratton Audley road w new council houses and the tower in the 1950s (Sue C

The CHURCH OF ENGLAND PRIMARY SCHOOL was opened in 1973 to replace the Old National School on the other side of the Green. There are nearly 120 children in the school now.

Turn left at the large chestnut tree and walk up the Stratton Audley Road.

The corner by the School opposite Laurels Farm used to be known as 'Jackman's Garden', after Albert Jackman, the farrier. Early in the 1900s there was an old cottage here, with two large willow trees in the garden. Mrs Blencowe, Gladys Hinks's grandmother, used to live here.

SUNNYSIDE was the site of the smithy, where Albert Jackman worked until his death in 1951. Ernest Perrin bought it in 1953, when he left the Old Forge, and he ran it with his brother. When it closed in the 1960s, Jack Wise bought the building and used it as a storeroom.

The house next door used to be called Sunnyside and it was the home of Phyllis and Arthur Omar after the War. Phyllis, whose sister Ivy ran the pub in Hethe, had a shop here for many years before Jack Wise bought it. Dick Wise took it over from his brother when he had problems with it, and let his daughter, Sue Gahan, run it with help from her sister, Ann Blake. Bill and Sue Jones took it on for the last year before it closed in the late 1970s. The house was rebuilt in the 1980s.

The CRICKET GROUND, on the left, was presented to the village by Henry Chinnery. The Cricket Club will be celebrating its centenary in 2001, although in Candleford Green in the 1890s the rector, Mr Delafield, is said to have put cricket 'upon a proper footing, with an eleven of young men and practice nights for boys'.[9] By 1915, at the latest, there was also a women's eleven!

The BUTCHERS ARMS is listed as seventeenth and eighteenth century and it was definitely licensed by 1735. In 1774 there was a Bricklayers Arms in the village - possibly the same inn. Albert Green ran the pub from 1913 to 1955! He also ran a taxi service. It is very different today where the pub has had five landlords in six years. Albert's son, Phil, still lives in one of the council houses.

The MALT HOUSE, behind the pub, dates from the eighteenth century or earlier. The trophy cabinet in the back room of the pub used to be a doorway through to the Malt House. Two families, the Bryants and the Franktons (Mrs Timms's parents), used to live here. There used to be another smithy up Green Lane, the path on the north side. For many years the gypsies used to camp here every summer.

The COUNCIL HOUSES in Wise Crescent and on the Stratton Audley Road were built in the early 1950s. They had all the modern conveniences, which represented a major advance in the standard of housing in the village. Initially, weekly rents for the two-bedroomed type were 15s. (75p) inclusive of rates. By 1958 rents were 18s. (90p), with rates an extra 4s.11d. (25p) plus 1s. 3d. (6p) for an electric cooker. In the 1990s all the houses in the Stratton Audley Road were modernised and refaced.

Walk back past the cricket ground to the large chestnut tree.

LAURELS FARM, on the corner, is listed as late seventeenth or early eighteenth century but parts may be earlier. Some cellars and an old staircase survive. The Wise family were farming here from 1939 and before them Thomas Gibbard and his sister Elizabeth. George Gibbard was farming here in 1861 and probably earlier. There used to be an off-licence at the farm and people remember sitting on the wall by the Green with their drinks. During the War they used to drink in the air-raid shelter, which had been dug in the garden. The new houses in the Laurels were built when the farmland was sold in the 1980s. In the 1990s, Richard Wise built a new house called Laurels Farm on the back road to Caversfield.

GREEN FARM is listed as late seventeenth century with eighteenth-century additions. Parts, including an old floor, may be earlier. The west end is a separate dwelling. The Wilkins family (Myrtle Ayris's parents) and the Hancocks were living here in the 1940s. The farm was left to the Tew family by John Dewar-Harrison in 1967 and old Mr Tew lived in the west end until his death.

Top left: The Cottage in the 1950s before it was rebuilt by Roy Ayris (Judy Legg)

Top right: The Old Bakehouse and the village pond in 1912 (Bill Plumb)

Middle left: The Old Bakehouse with Myrtle Wilkins and the three Gough sisters crossing the Green in the 1940s (Village Hall)

Middle Right: Albert Price with his pony and trap in St Michael's Close in the 1970s. Rosalind Marsh is on the pony. Others include: Tina Jones, Nick Wise, Neil Wickens and Carol Bond (Sue Gahan)

Bottom: Main Street in the 1920s, possibly showing Albert Price's motor bike and side-car in the foreground. Folly Barn is on the right and part of Mansfield Yard in the distance (Gordon Allen)

Fringford, Bicester.

Fringford Oxon

THE COTTAGE was sold by John Dewar-Harrison 'for a song and a handshake' (as were a number of other properties in the village!) to Roy and Myrtle Ayris in the late 1950s. It was an old seventeenth- or eighteenth-century thatched cottage, which Roy, with much local help, rebuilt almost completely. Lena Knibbs was living here in the 1940s.

CROW LANE was the old name for the lane leading to the Hethe road, as there used to be elm trees on both sides full of crows. There were gardens on the west side, some of them used by the Old School.

The 'Bridge Ground' ALLOTMENTS used to be on the left of the Hethe road before Fringford Bridge. An 1899 plan of these allotments, with a schedule of allotment rentals, survives. There were 65 allotments of varying sizes, with rentals from 2s.1d. (10p) to 5s.3d. (26p) per half year, payable on Lady Day and Michaelmas. There were also some allotments known as 'Crabdy (or Crabtree) Piece' on the right of the back road near Waterloo Farm. They were all given up in the 1950s.

The OLD BAKEHOUSE dates from the seventeenth century. Harold Crook was the baker between the Wars. He used to wear a cape and a big black hat, which scared the children! In those days the baker would still roast Sunday joints for the villagers for 2d or 3d. Bert Hancock from Green Farm ran the bakery after Mr Crook sold it, followed by Mr Newby. Les Morgan was the last man to run the bakery and he is still remembered for the quality of his cakes! He and his wife moved to Stratton Audley to run the post office in the late 1960s. Ancil Rawlinson's father lived in the house from 1976 to 1986. By mutual agreement, he took the pond over from the village and cleaned it up.

The OLD SCHOOL was built as a National (i.e. Church of England) School in 1866 by the rector, Henry de Salis, on land leased from John Dewar-Harrison. This was the site of the sixteenth-century North Manor occupied by the Wenmans, and later of the parish Poor House, known as 'The Barracks' (pulled down about 1830). The South Manor was probably on the site of Moat Farm (formerly Cotmore Farm). The Old School was used as a Victorian Study Centre after the school transferred to the new site in 1973. It is no longer in use and there are plans to sell the site for development. The local playgroup still uses the wooden hut.

The OLD SCHOOL HOUSE was built in 1876 on land leased from Lord Sidmouth. Edwin Blackburn and his wife, who were the first teachers in the National School, were the first occupants. The headteachers lived here until 1964. Note that the doorways to the toilets for the old school can still be seen in the outer garden wall.

COTTAGES ON THE GREEN: Nos.1 and 2 were built about 1960, nos.3 and 4 about 1950 and nos.5 and 6 in 1929. Albert White used to live in no.6. He always smoked a pipe, grew his own tobacco and hung it out in the attic - the smell is still remembered! For many years Albert Price lived in Rose Cottage, an old thatched cottage on the site of no.1.

Albert, known as 'Noah', was a legendary character in the village. The nickname seems to have arisen because one of his sheds, like the Ark, was in a field which was almost totally under water. He was a painter/decorator, like others in the Price family. He rode an old motorbike with a sidecar, in which he kept his ladder and all his decorating equipment. It was only on rare occasions that this equipment seems to have been used. He was a great talker and, as one builder used to say 'Lock him in and keep him in'! Otherwise no work was done. When he was commissioned by Albert Green to redecorate the pub, he painted one room and then left and did not return! He had at least three small sheds (or 'farms' as he called them) in various places in the parish. He kept his horse in one of them, next to The Cottage. On occasion, when his wife was asked where Albert was, she would reply 'I don't know. On Top Farm, Middle Farm or Lower Farm'! He and his horse can be seen in one of the photographs, drawing the coffin at John Dewar-Harrison's funeral in 1967.

SPRING HOUSE was built very recently on part of the garden of no.6, where there used to be a pump.

HALL FARM (formerly Fringford Hall) is listed as early seventeenth century with eighteenth- and twentieth-century alterations. Part of the north end may date from the fourteenth century. The two-storey addition on the south-west side was built in the late seventeenth century. A brick dovecote survives at the rear between the ground and first floors.

The Addington family have owned the farm for some 400 years, although the family have not lived there since 1746. Dr Anthony Addington was doctor to William Pitt the Elder (the Earl of Chatham) and to George III during his 'madness'. In 1788 he was the only doctor to successfully predict the king's recovery from what is now known to have been porphyria. His son, Henry, became Speaker and Prime Minister (1801-4) and the first Lord Sidmouth. He is also remembered as the minister who introduced Income Tax. For much of the nineteenth century and the first half of the twentieth century the Mansfield family farmed here. Lovell Buckingham took over from them in the late 1930s and farmed it until Ian Thomas arrived in the 1960s.

The OLD FORGE is listed as mid-eighteenth century with twentieth-century alterations. It also used to be the sub-post office, where Flora Thompson worked as assistant postmistress from 1891 to 1897.
In Flora's time the forge and the post office were both run by Kesia Whitton (*Dorcas Lane* in the book). Kesia's husband, John, died shortly after Flora's arrival. Both of them were very large, as you can see in one of the photographs. He weighed over 22 stone and Kesia over 18 stone. When she died in 1898, Frederick Plumb, who was one of the blacksmiths, had to take out the left hand upstairs bedroom window so that her heavy coffin could be lowered down a ladder; it was too big to carry down the stairs. You can still see where he subsequently patched up the window with a plate. The Whittons' maid, Zilpha Hinks (*Zillah* in the book), died in 1900 and her grave is in the churchyard.
After Kesia Whitton's death, Frederick Plumb took over the tenancy. The post office was moved to Rectory Lane, where it was run first by James Wyatt and then by Ernest and Elsie Price. The Plumbs purchased the property in 1923 for £500 and members of the family continued to live there until the 1990s. Ernest Perrin rented the forge after Frederick Plumb died in 1930 and continued the business until he bought the other farrier's shop in 1953. The Automobile Association sign on the front of the house was originally put up in about 1926; it was common at the time to put these signs up on village forges. Along with all signposts, it was taken down in the War. Bill Plumb found it in a shed after the War and put it back up.

MIDWAY was built by Bill Plumb in the early 1970s in the orchard of The Old Forge, where his father, William, was still living.

KOHANKA, on the other side of the street, is on the site of two old thatched cottages, where Bill Hitchcock and Harry Batchelor used to live. Bill worked at Hall Farm, Harry on the Shelswell Estate as a stonemason.

ROSEMARY COTTAGE was built in 1952 on the site of an old thatched cottage. Mr Smith and Jimmy Gerring, the sexton for many years, used to live here.

The Post Office and the Forge in the early 1890s, with Mr and Mrs Whitton standing by the cart. William Elderfield, the watchmender, is standing on far left with sledgehammer on his shoulder; Frederick Plumb, blacksmith, is third from left (Bill Plumb)

Frederick Plumb driving his gig with his sister, Bel, in the early 1900s (Bill Plumb)

GANDERS is on the site of the old thatched cottage where Bill Grantham's parents lived at one time and where he was born. Bill's father, William, was a carrier and later a coal merchant until he retired in 1936. He kept his cart and, later, his coal lorry in a barn on the corner of Church Lane. The Granthams have had the longest family connection with the village, stretching back some 400 years. In 1847, Bill's great-grandfather, James Grantham, was keeping the Butchers Arms and he was also a baker. His son, James, became a carrier, going to Banbury, Bicester, Brackley and Buckingham every week.

Bill likes to imagine the hard times, which his family and many others must have had during the agricultural depressions in the nineteenth century. In May 1884, for example, the local newspaper recorded that James's wife, Sarah, was in court for stealing butter in Bicester. The chairman, W.W.M.Dewar, took a lenient view of the offence and she was given 21 days hard labour in Oxford. Apparently, he could have given her three months in prison with hard labour!

ROSECROFT is the only eighteenth-century cottage to survive on this side of Main Street. Cecil and Agnes Cross used to live here. Cecil was the butcher and his Slaughter House was next door on the corner of what is now Crosslands. Agnes was the church organist for many years. Fred Mansfield lived in a small cottage on the other side of Rosecroft.

GABLE COTTAGE originally was two eighteenth-century cottages. An 1818 datestone on the rear part may be the date of some later alterations. Note that the gable-end fronts onto Main Street. This was common where there was limited frontage available on the main street and a cottage had to be squeezed into a very narrow space. It is interesting to note on the gable-end the steep pitch of the original thatched roof. Les Golder, who is a member of another old Fringford family, has lived here since the 1930s. Walter Blake used to live in the rear cottage.

STONE GAP COTTAGE is part of a line of four cottages, with The Cottage (no.6), Fox Cottage (formerly Amberley) and Bakery Cottage. They are all listed as mid-eighteenth century, although they may be older. The porches were added in the twentieth century. The row of cottages was owned at one time by Thomas Allen from Fringford Mill, and later by the Buckinghams. Stone Gap was the old sweet and cigarette shop run by "Lizzie" Grantham, Bill's aunt, from the 1930s until she retired in the late 1950s. Bill recalls that she used to put her hand on the scales

Rosecroft, formerly home of Cecil Cross the butcher, with the butcher's shop on the right (Stephanie Maciejewski)

to make sure that she never gave them too many sweets! Lizzie's two sisters, Mrs Slatter and Mrs Wise, lived in Amberley and Bakery Cottage. Gilbert Slatter was a stonemason and built Stonehaven further down Main Street. Earlier, James Grantham, the carrier, lived in Amberley. On the left of the house is the old cart entrance with wide plank doors, where he used to keep his horse and cart.

FRINGFORD COTTAGE was built in 1938 by Miss Joyce Tomkinson. She was related to the Goslings of Stratton Audley and more distantly to the Palmer-Tomkinson family. She was a great character and played a leading part in village life, as Chair of the Parish Council, Chair of Managers of the School and President of the Cricket Club. She was greatly loved and a little feared by the village. She rode side-saddle to hounds until her early 70s and never missed a meet until a few months before her death.

FOLLY FIELDS was the site of Folly Barn, which belonged to the Sumners at Church Farm until after the Second World War. The Buckingham family bought the barn and built the house here.

FOLLY COTTAGES date from the eighteenth century. The present two cottages were once a line of three smaller thatched cottages and you can see where some of the old doorways have been filled in. You can also see some alterations to the south wall. The porches were added in the twentieth century.

Evacuees lived in no.1 during the Second World War, including Jack and Win Mirams and their son John. Mr and Mrs Dick Cadd lived in no.2 with their son. Mr and Mrs Dudley and their family lived in no.3. He was a butcher in Twyford and he used to walk there and back each day to work! Later, Daisy Judd (nanny to Ellis Chinnery in Fringford House) and Mabel Judd lived here. The Judd sisters had been born at Church Farm, where the family lived for many years. Nos.2 and 3 have romance attached to them, as they were made into one after Chris Singleton (no.3) married Jane (no.2) in the late 1970s. This caused some confusion for the milkman among others!

BEAGLE COTTAGE dates from the eighteenth century. Jean Winters lives here now. Her father, Fred Cooper, used to live next door in part of Lilac Cottage, where Jean and her sister were born. Previous occupants have included Mrs Batchelor, Gladys and Tom Blake, Elsie and Fred Reeves and the Lawrence family.

LILAC COTTAGE is listed as early eighteenth century and used to be three cottages; there are still three old staircases. It has been renovated recently and you can see where some of the old doorways have been blocked up. The Cooper family lived in the end one for many years. Previous occupants have included Mrs Liza Judd, Mr and Mrs George White and Mrs Richardson, a former Head of the Old School.

HOLLY COTTAGE (formerly Stonehaven) was built by Gilbert Slatter on the site of an old thatched cottage. Mr and Mrs Bywater used to live in the old cottage, when he was the gardener at the Old Rectory in Hethe. Bill and Hannah Grantham lived here in the 1940s for a rent of 3 shillings (15p) per week and had no electricity until 1948. In 1891 another member of the Judd family, Thomas a coal haulier, was living here.

ST MICHAEL'S CLOSE was developed in the late 1960s on the site of the old MANSFIELD YARD. There used to be a group of old cottages here, all of which were demolished, except Yew Tree Cottage. The Yard was commonly known as "Birdie Cage" after Margaret Bird, who owned most of the cottages.

Mansfield Yard with Yew Tree Cottage (former home of the Hinks) on the right. The Elderfields lived next door (Gladys Hinks)

Granny Elizabeth Hinks with her lace bobbins, sitting with Mr Spacey in Mansfield Yard c.1900 (Gladys Hinks)

William Elderfield, who had a thriving clock and watch repair business, lived in one of the cottages and had a separate workshop in the Yard. He used to do repairs for Harrods in London in addition to all his local work. Older residents recall the hundreds of pounds' worth of clocks and watches ticking away in his workshop. William was a blacksmith when he joined the army during the First World War. His delicate touch was discovered then and he was trained as a watchmaker.

YEW TREE COTTAGE was built by David Mansfield in the late nineteenth century and his name is still carved above the fireplace. Ernest and Emily Hinks used to live here with their daughter, Gladys, as did her grandparents, Henry and Elizabeth, before them. Emily, and later Gladys, ran a small shop. The cottage has since been enlarged. Ernest, who was a carpenter by trade, also kept pigs and hens in a paddock leased from John Dewar-Harrison next to the Yard. After the First World War, when it was very difficult to find employment, Ernest used to 'get on his bike' and cycle to Coventry to look for work. During the Second World War he was a ganger employed by the RAF, to do all sorts of 'rural jobs' on the Shelswell airfield.

The VILLAGE PUMP opposite Mansfield Yard was for use by the Church end of the village until the arrival of mains water in about 1960. However, the pump water was infected by the trees, so people used water from the wells for drinking. There were a great number of wells in the village, including no less than three at the Old Forge. The thatched cover was put over the pump in memory of Douglas Crowther, who died in 1987.

THE LODGE was built in the Gothic style by Mr Chinnery in 1898, when he was rebuilding Fringford Manor. Jim Wyatt lived here with his family when he took over the tenancy of Manor Farm just before the Second World War. His grandson, Mark, lives there now. Just beyond the Lodge there used to be two sets of gates at the entrances to the Manor.

FRINGFORD MANOR was converted from a farmhouse in 1899-1900 by Henry Chinnery, who leased the property from John Dewar-Harrison. In 1948 Dewar-Harrison wanted to build new houses for some of his workers. When he found that this was impossible because of shortages after the War, he converted the Manor into six houses for them. There were more conversions in the 1980s, to the west barns, where the Manor's milking parlour had been, and in the stable yard. In no.6,

Fringford Manor in 1922 showing the fine front garden (Bill Plumb)

Laura Powell ran the post office (said to be the smallest one in England) from 1949 to 1986, after the Prices in Rectory Lane retired.

During the Second World War a convent junior school was evacuated to the Manor. The senior school was evacuated to Swift's House, Stoke Lyne. Norah Morgan recalls how both schools used to walk in crocodile every Sunday to the Catholic church in Hethe; the juniors in dark brown uniforms, the seniors in dark blue ones.

MANOR FARM was built by John Wyatt in the 1980s, on the site of the Manor's kitchen garden and orchard. His father had inherited the farm and adjoining land from John Dewar-Harrison in 1967. The Manor Road houses were also built in the old orchard in the 1980s. Manor Farm is now a herb farm.

Walk down to the end of the road into the courtyard.

This is where the coachman and other staff lived and the carriages, and later the cars, were garaged. The grooms' messroom and the tack room (Coach House Cottage) were on the right next to the carriage rooms (the Coach House). Straight ahead is the Gardener's Cottage, where Mr Crowe used to live. The converted Old Stables are on the left.

Walk back to the churchyard and enter.

The Churchyard was enlarged in 1875 and 1906 by gifts of land from Eton College and the Harrison family. The War Memorial on the left records the names of the five men who gave their lives in the First World War (see chapter 5). The unusual castiron crosses, which you can see over a number of the graves, date from 1888 to 1937. Research has shown that there are more such crosses in Fringford (24) than anywhere else in Oxfordshire, and that 5 of them were made at Stratford on Avon by John Smith. These castiron crosses were available nationally in various forms and they were very popular, because they were much cheaper than stone memorials.[10]

ST MICHAEL'S AND ALL ANGELS CHURCH stands on the site of an early wooden building, which may have served the Saxon villagers for hundreds of years. The earliest part of the present stone church dates from the early twelfth century, when Baron Manessah Arsic built a new church and granted it to the priory of Black Monks, instituted at Cogges, near Witney, by his father. The south door, although much restored, dates from this period, as do the two northern arches of the nave.

Thirteenth century: On the south side of the nave, there are some men's heads carved on one pillar making faces at some grotesque women's heads on the opposite pillar. These seem to be a thirteenth-century carver's joke!

Sixteenth century: The roughly carved medieval screen dates from this period.

Eighteenth century: There are two memorials to the Addington family of Hall Farm on the wall of the north aisle.

Nineteenth century: The church was largely rebuilt in this period. From 1814 to 1894, Fringford was fortunate to enjoy the considerable personal wealth, intellectual ability and social standing of three 'regal rectors': Henry Roundell, Henry de Salis and Cadwallader Coker. All three are commemorated in the church.

In 1821, a new chancel was built, in 1829 the north aisle was rebuilt and in 1831 the present stone tower was built to replace the wooden belfry. In 1842, the pulpit was installed, using seventeenth-century panels from neighbouring Hardwick Manor, and the vestry was built. In 1857, the south aisle was enlarged under the guidance of the diocesan architect, G.E.Street.

There are two fonts in the south aisle, an octagonal one possibly from the fifteenth century, presented by Henry Roundell, and a round one of 1880 in memory of Anne King, whose family lived at Waterloo Farm. Beneath the bell ropes there is a wheeled handbier for use at 'walking funerals', which was presented by the King family in 1912.

Twentieth century: In 1905, the north chapel was rebuilt by the Chinnery family and two clerestory windows were added. The wall painting, behind the altar, may also have been commissioned then. In 1909, the roof was restored. The fine altar in the north aisle was given by Mrs Marjorie Chinnery in 1972. Some local people still refer to the north aisle as the 'Chinnery chapel'. The Chinnery graves are at the back of the church, outside the north chapel.

The Carvings: In 1839, John Rogers, the organist and village carpenter, carved new seats for the nave. He also made the fine casing for the organ, which was given by Henry de Salis in 1853. The beautiful carving on the pew-ends was done after the First World War by Charlie Freeman, who lived on the Green. He had been severely disabled by frostbite in Canada and did much of his work lying down in the aisles. He also carved the whole vestry wall and the choir-stalls.

The Stained Glass: There was so much stained glass installed in the nineteenth century that, as a later rector said, 'no one can now read his prayer book without electric light'! The Roundell family filled all the windows in the chancel. In the north aisle, one window is dedicated to Cadwallader Coker and his family and another one to John Dewar, who was killed in the Boer War in 1900.

The Bells: One of the bells was cast by R.Atton of Buckingham in 1617 and two of them by R.Chandler in 1702. The small Sanctus bell was cast by Robert Wills of Aldbourne, Wiltshire about 1800.

There have been few alterations to the church since the nineteenth century. Not surprisingly restoration is now much-needed and £50,000 is being raised for this purpose. The church is one of ten in the Shelswell Group of Churches in the Diocese of Oxford, which are now combined under one rector, Ricky Yates.

Leave the churchyard by the small gate at the north-west corner.

As you leave, note the memorial on the right to the Revd Coker and members of his family, including his son, Lewis, who died at Ekowe in 1879, aged 19. He was serving as a midshipman in the Naval Brigade on HMS Active during the Anglo-Zulu Wars. Most of the Coker family are commemorated in St Edburg's Church in Bicester.

CHURCH FARM HOUSE (formerly Eton College Farm) was probably an old timber-framed farmhouse in the sixteenth century and there may well have been earlier farm buildings on the site, which belonged to Eton College. By the late nineteenth century, the farmhouse had been converted into cottages. The Judd family, who were mostly agricultural labourers and coal hauliers, lived here from about 1860 until 1921, as tenants of the Waters family who leased the farm from the College. In 1921, the College sold the farm to Harold Judd, when they were selling all their remaining property in Fringford and Cottisford. Unfortunately Harold had to sell the property almost immediately, as he had run into difficulties with his electrical business.

In 1928, the Sumners bought it and owned it until 1965, by which time the property was in a very poor state of repair. During much of this period the house was divided into three cottages with a dairy. The house was restored in the late 1960s and made into one dwelling again. The remains of the old granary were pulled down in the late 1980s, when an annexe for grooms was built on the south end. The annexe has now been incorporated into the main house, the old stables have been largely rebuilt and the old cowshed restored.

The Judd family had a long connection with the village from at least the early nineteenth century. Thomas Judd was the parish clerk for thirty-seven years from the late 1860s for the princely fee of £5 p.a. The churchwardens' accounts show that he did a variety of other tasks for the church. In 1874, for example, he supplied coal, gravel, wood and straw at a cost of £1.8s.0d. (£1.40), swept the flues and rang the bells. He used to collect coal from Finmere station and store it in bunkers in the farmyard. The remains of the bunkers and some lumps of coal were found in 1990 when some of the stables were removed. Thomas's son, Reuben, succeeded him as clerk and on his death in 1914, two of the Judd brothers took over from him.

*Owen Judd in front of Church Farm
in 1920 (Vera Raby)*

*Church Close looking towards the Church and
Church Farm c.1965 (Anthony Rickett)*

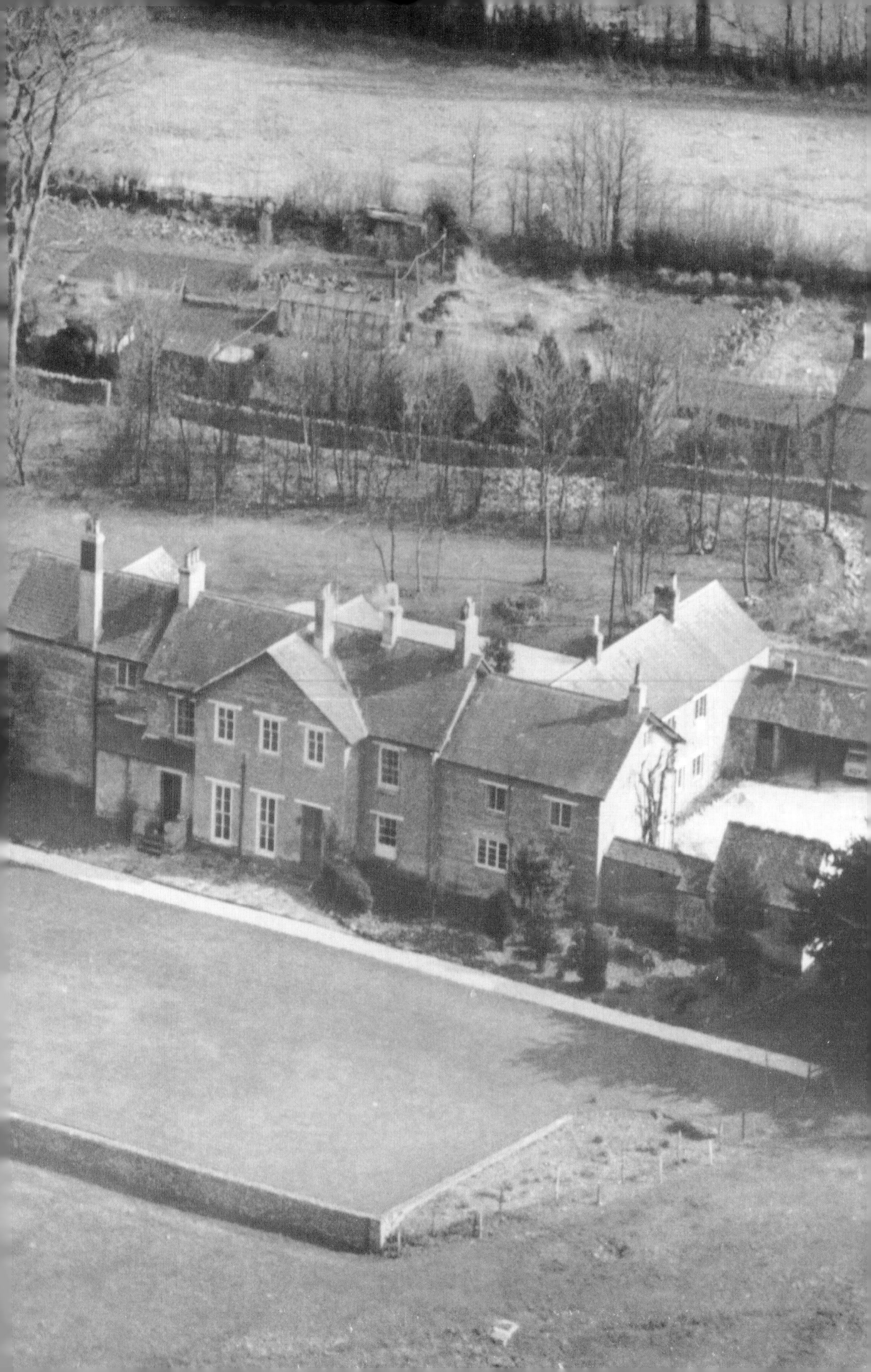

The family link did not end with the sale of the farm in 1921, although Harold moved to London and Owen to King's Sutton, where he became a coal merchant. Daisy and Mabel Judd, two of Harold's sisters, spent much of their lives in the village, living together in Mansfield Yard and then in Folly Cottages. Daisy, always known as 'Nanny Judd', had returned from being in service in Chester to be nanny to Ellis Chinnery's family on Rectory Lane. She was a powerful character and by all accounts told Mrs Chinnery exactly what to do with the children!

CHURCH LANE As a result of the changes in occupancy over the last 150 years, the lane has been variously called Judds Lane, Sumners Lane and now Church Lane.

ROSEMARY COTTAGE is a late Victorian cottage built by the rector, Cadwallader Coker. George 'Snobby' Judd, a shoemaker and an older brother of Reuben, lived here until his death in 1935.

FORGE MILL HOUSE was built in 1990-91 by Paddy McMahon, after he sold Church Farm House. It was named after his famous horse, Pennwood Forge Mill.

CHURCH COTTAGES nos.1 and 2 are late Victorian cottages, built by the Revd Coker. No.2 has been extended recently. The property was conveyed to the Chinnery family in 1900.

Take the small footpath on the right after Church Cottages.

GHOST LANE is an apt name for what was a rather spooky path in earlier days. Was there an old drovers' road here leading on past the church? Does a shepherd still walk the lane? Is there a ghost from the Civil War skirmish near Fringford in March 1645, when the Royalists were retreating from Finmere? The explanation is probably more mundane. This was the route for 'walking funerals' on the handbier from the undertaker, Billy Judd on Rectory Lane, to the church.

Notice the long garden on the left. It was here that all the cottages in Prentice Yard used to have their gardens. On the right is the long boundary wall of the Old Rectory garden.

The OLD RECTORY in 1756 was a mere thatched cottage, too small for the rector's family. It was enlarged by the Revd Roundell in 1817-18 for £2098, when he added

Aerial view of the Old Rectory and the
Prentice Yard gardens in 1976 (Charles Hebditch)

the larger rooms on the east side and refaced the whole house with local stone. The kitchen and laundry were in the earlier west wing of the house, with the stables and coach-house. There is now a separate occupant in part of the west wing. Note the old bell on the roof, which may have been used to call the children to their lessons, when there was a school in the barn next door.

The drive to the Rectory used to go round the back of Bancroft, which was an orchard, and up to the old front of the house. Traces of the old front door and doorstep can still be seen, where there is a curve in the stonework. A cart track used to cross the Bull Field (formerly known as Bancroft) and connect the Rectory with the Hethe road. The large garden and the broad view over towards Willaston are to be admired. There are also some fine trees, planted by Roundell and his successors, and a substantial walled garden.

BANCROFT was built for the Standens in 1964, when Jack Standen retired as headteacher of the Old School and moved out of the Old School House. The old barn on the right, together with the Bancroft property, used to be owned by the Church, and there used to be other old outbuildings on the property. In 1853, the Revd de Salis noted 'No school room. Half of the Old Tithe Barn fitted up by me as a School House for which purpose it now answers very well'. There were 35 children here and 20 at an infant school, until the National School was built in 1866.[11] The Standens sold the house to the Woods in 1978.

Rectory Lane in the 1930s with Frank Sumner, Bill Blake, Arthur Alger and Gladys Hinks (Bill Plumb)

RECTORY LANE (formerly known simply as 'The Other Street') is a very old road, which was probably used by drovers in Saxon times. They used to take their sheep to Brackley, which was a thriving wool centre. The old lane went round to the left of the Bancroft property and continued across the field down to 'Fera's Ford' and up to Willaston. There were still traces of a stone paved way to Willaston in the nineteenth century. The young Flora Timms would have taken this route from the post office up to Shelswell Manor in the 1890s.

FRINGFORD HOUSE on the right dates in part from the seventeenth century, while the two wings were added in the mid-nineteenth century. Ellis and Katharine Chinnery used to live here.

CANDLEFORD MEWS includes the Pump House and the Coach House, which used to be stables and outbuildings for Fringford House. When Katharine Chinnery died in 1978, they were converted and Candleford Cottage was built at the end of the Mews.

MEADOW VIEW, opposite the Rectory gates, was part of a row of five cottages built in the eighteenth century or earlier. The brick second storey seems to have been added later. This was the home of Billy Judd, the undertaker, who was also chauffeur to the Chinnerys at the Manor and a carpenter/handyman. Billy was a great village character, who is remembered as a 'loveable rogue' and a great drinker, who could be too clever for his own good! There was nothing mechanical or electrical that he could not fix. He had the first wireless in the village and used to charge up batteries for others. He drove his own Bullnose Morris, one of the first cars in the village. He could be extremely smart, whether dressed as the undertaker or chauffeuring the Chinnerys.

THE YARD was formerly known as PRENTICE YARD, after William Prentice, a butcher from Bicester, who bought it from Thomas Gibbard of Laurels Farm in April 1902 for £310. The group of nine cottages had also been sold as a block in 1875 when it was known as Franklin's Yard. The Yard used to have another row of three or four cottages on the edge of the lane. The first one was a grocery shop, remembered as 'Mrs Carey's', where there used to be a chocolate machine on a post outside the shop. She died just before the Second World War but Miss Hutton and then the Savins continued to run the shop. The row of cottages was demolished when Prentice Yard was split up in the early 1950s.

'Granny Wright' had a small sweet shop in part of what is now STABLE COTTAGE (formerly Samarkand). The House family occupied the rear of the cottage. Eb Sirett and Edie Price lived next door. Behind them there were two cottages occupied by the Cherry and Timms families. MAVIS HOUSE, which was also part of the group, has now been modernised and extended on the right-hand end.

LITTLE PADDOCK is a mid-1990s development.

PUMP COTTAGE is named after the pump, which was used by the residents on Rectory Lane and by the Old School. Old Mrs James used to live here.

VIXEN COTTAGE used to be occupied by the Priest family. Note the blocked door and window still visible on the north wall and some alterations to the south wall. There used to be two other small stone cottages on the south side. One was occupied by the Smith family, who were Joan Hawes's parents; the other by Miss Hitchcock, who ran a small shop. Henry Taylor demolished the cottages, after he had bought them with the two brick cottages next door for £100 each. He apparently needed the stone to build some walls.

BOND'S COTTAGES next door, end on to the Lane, are much altered. They used to be two old cottages, occupied by the Whites & Albert Jackman, the farrier.

FARRIERS CLOSE, which originally would have been part of the Green, is the latest development in the village, built at the end of the 1990s. Excavations prior to the development revealed a series of Iron Age and Romano-British boundary ditches. These were overlain by a further series of ditches of the tenth or eleventh century, including a possible domestic enclosure. This phase was superseded in the twelfth century by ridge-and-furrow arable activity. This continued until the second half of the thirteenth century, when three stone buildings were constructed. One of these appears to have been a farrier's workshop. It is possible that the buildings formed part of a manorial complex. In the middle of the fourteenth century the buildings appear to have been abandoned and the whole area converted to pasture. This was the period of the Black Death and other plagues, which resulted in large-scale depopulation.

PRINGLE COTTAGE was probably built in the eighteenth century. The south end and the bay window were added in the 1950s and at the same time the north end, which used to be a workshop, was converted. Ernest and Elsie Price used to run the post office here from about 1910 until 1949. Ernest also worked as a plumber. There used to be a post-box and later a telephone kiosk by the front gate. Members of the Price family lived here and next door in Rose Cottage from the 1860s. They rented the copse across the road by the Old School House as a garden. Mrs Standen's sisters, Gertie and Gladys Preedy, lived here in the 1960s.

Many of the Price family were plumbers, painters, decorators and general builders. By a lucky chance some of their old ledgers survived in the attic of Pringle Cottage. They provide a fascinating record of their customers and work from 1869 until the early 1900s. Albert Price was one of their sons.

ROSE COTTAGE was originally a thatched cottage, probably built in the eighteenth century. During the Second World War Sam Goddard, a schoolmaster who came with the evacuees, lived in one half. Lily Price was living in the other half. She was the infants' teacher in the 1940s, when she was described by Mr Corfe as having no qualifications and being a bit temperamental. But he also thought that she was 'a solid worker who does jolly well!'[12]

You can now retrace your steps to the Green where you started your stroll.

Fringford Church, Bicester

Chapter 3

Church and Clergy

There has been a church on the present site since Saxon times, although the earliest part of the present stone church dates from the early twelfth century. There is limited information about the early rectors but we do have a continuous list of names from 1565 (see Appendix 2). The most interesting of them is John Bayley, a Presbyterian, who was made minister in 1645 during the Civil War. He replaced William Overton, who was deposed for refusing to accept the Act of Parliament abolishing the Book of Common Prayer. In 1648 Bayley, together with Samuel Wells, the Presbyterian Minister of Banbury, went to London to petition for the King's life. For his courage he was himself deposed but allowed to live on in Fringford until the restoration of Charles II in 1660. He was then reappointed rector of Fringford and served as a loyal Anglican until 1697. He and his wife are both buried in Fringford.

From the middle of the eighteenth century to the end of the nineteenth century, Fringford was particularly fortunate in its rectors. John Russell Greenhill (1756-1813) was a cousin of the Russell family, who owned Chequers in Buckinghamshire before it was given to the nation for our Prime Ministers. He himself had a large estate at Ellesborough, near Chequers. Although he never lived in the village, as the rectory was too small for a family, he took a great interest in it. In 1767, he moved from Croydon to Finmere and from 1773, he lived in Cottisford, where he bought the lease of Cottisford House. Two of his manuscript diaries survive, in which he entered his daily engagements and recorded meticulous weather observations. These records show him to have been unusually conscientious, in a period when there were many absentee and pluralist parsons who never visited their parishes. The entries also give the reader an interesting insight into the daily life of an eighteenth-century parson.

The Church c.1900 (Bill Plumb)

For the next 80 years after Greenhill, Fringford was fortunate to enjoy considerable benefits from three distinguished 'regal rectors'. The attractions of such a small rural village for them are not immediately obvious. However, the Crown had taken over the advowson, the right to present the rector, in 1766 and by 1817 the annual tithes and stipends were some £431. This was a good sum in those days and compares, for example, to less than £120 for the vicars of Fritwell. Henry Roundell (1814-52) came from a great Yorkshire family and possessed ample means and a genial temperament. He enlarged the rectory and was responsible for the rebuilding of the chancel and much of the other restoration of the church. He also let out part of the glebe as allotments for the labourers, which was a rare kindness at that time.[13] In 1846 he became the first Rural Dean of the Bicester Deanery. In 1848, he was described by his churchwardens as very sober, his dress gentlemanly and becoming a minister,[14] although Bishop Wilberforce found him 'a little huffish'![15] There seems to have been a genuine affection for him in the parish and when Wilberforce spoke at his funeral in 1852, there were 'many wet eyes'.[16]

Henry Fane de Salis (1852-73) was another rector of ample means, the son of an Italian Count and son-in-law of J.W.Henley, who was a Cabinet Minister in the 1850s. He, too, contributed significantly to the restoration of the church. He became Diocesan Inspector but resigned from Fringford in 1873 on succeeding to property at Portnell Park, near Virginia Water. Cadwallader Coker (1873-94) was a member of a large and distinguished Bicester family, the owners of Bicester Hall. He had been rector of Shalstone, near Buckingham, for nineteen years and Rural Dean of Buckingham.

Top left: May Queen, Jean Faulkner, in the early 1950s, with the Revd Westlake and Jack Standen in the back row (Judy Legg)

Top right: The Friendly Society procession leaving the church on feast day, after the service, on its way to enjoy the entertainment on the Green c. 1900-10. Note Church Farm in the background (Bill Plumb)

Middle left: Leaving church after the service on Club Festival Day c.1900-10. Note the old gates and the elegant approach to the Manor (Bill Plumb)

Middle right: Family group outside the church in the 1920s. Mrs Mansfield senior is in the centre, George Mansfield with his wife on the right and Harry Batchelor with his wife, Amy Mansfield, second from the left (Gordon Allen)

Bottom: The Funeral Cortege of John Dewar-Harrison with Albert Price and his horse carrying the coffin through Newton Purcell in 1967 (Baroness von Maltzahn)

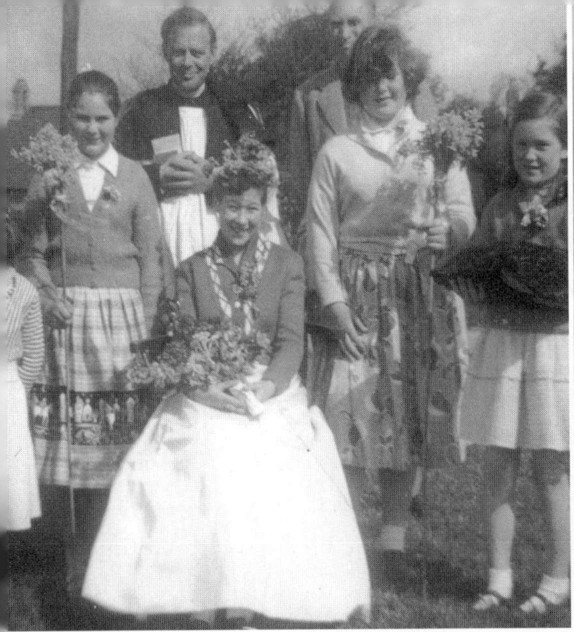
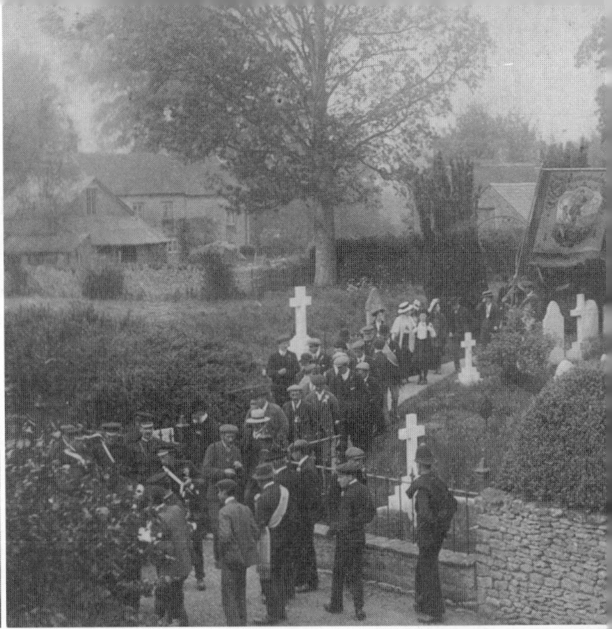
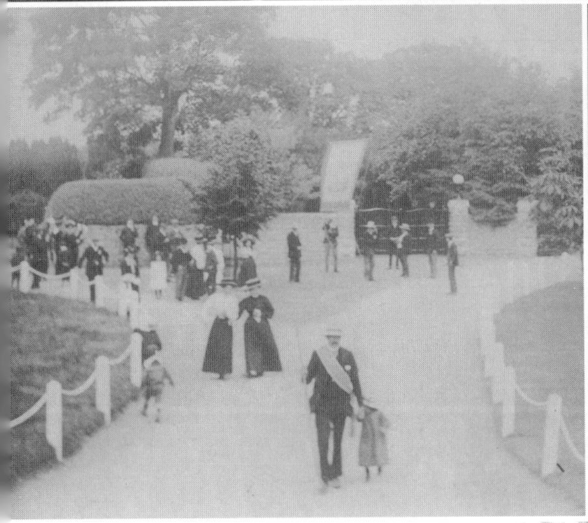
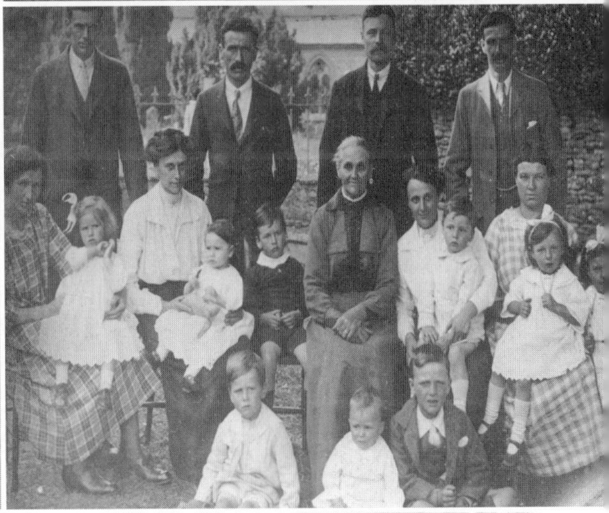
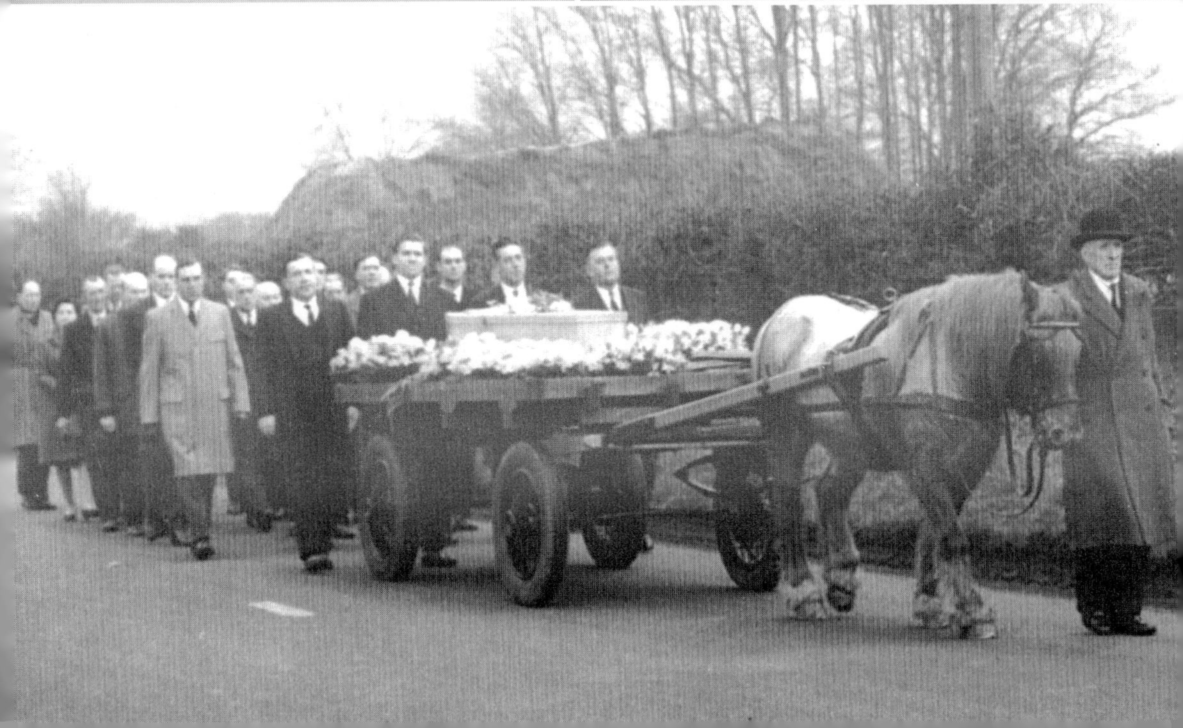

In 1894, democracy came with a bump to Fringford, with the arrival of Charles Thompson (1894-98). Flora Thompson vividly describes the consternation when the new rector (*Mr Delafield*) appeared in his shirtsleeves and helped the women carry their heavy faggots and laundry baskets, and turned the servants' hall at the Rectory into a Youth Club. 'Dignity did not enter into his composition' and some looked back to Coker and thought 'He was a gentleman, if ever there was one'![17] Charles Thompson, however, was very popular in the parish, partly because he had the reputation of being the best preacher in the neighbourhood, possibly in the county. They said his sermons 'made you feel two inches taller'.[18] It is not clear that this democracy continued with his successors, who seem to have been much more traditional. It is generally agreed locally that the next democratic leap forward did not come until the arrival of the Revd John Westlake (1954-63). He is remembered fondly for his gift of getting on with everybody, playing the piano and singing in the pub, and brewing his own wines.

Church attendance in Fringford during the nineteenth century seems to have compared favourably with that in other local churches. Greenhill found Fringford people 'very good frequenters' of their church, and in the 1851 religious census, estimated attendance was 130 in the morning and 200 in the afternoon. The pattern of services was changing, particularly the number of communion services. In 1805, there were only six a year, by 1817 they were monthly but it was not until the 1890s that weekly communion was celebrated. There were also celebrations on Great Festivals and Holy Days after about 1850. Attendance was variable and it decreased materially in the 1880s. However, in 1899 it was described as 'very satisfactory'. Sadly, it would be very difficult to make such a comment about any of the local churches in the year 2000.

The church itself is much as it was in the days when Flora Timms sat behind Mrs Slater-Harrison (*Lady Adelaide*) and noticed her perfume and the gracious dignity with which she knelt down. Only an avenue of prunus trees and a plaque in the porch have been added in memory of *Lady Adelaide's* nephew, Mr John Dewar-Harrison. He is remembered fondly by many local people, particularly by those tenant farmers who were left their farms in his will.

In 1924, the parishes of Fringford and Hethe were united. In 1983, the North and South Shelswell benefices were created, Fringford being in the southern one with

Godington, Hardwick-cum-Tusmore, Hethe and Stratton Audley. In 1995, when the Revd Anthony Hichens retired, the North benefice (Cottisford, Finmere, Mixbury, Newton Purcell and Stoke Lyne) was combined with the South, to form the Shelswell Group of ten churches under one rector, Ricky Yates.

Nonconformists

Fringford seems to have been loyal to the Church of England throughout its history, with few instances of Catholics, Methodists or other Nonconformists in the village. In the late eighteenth century, there was a small group of Presbyterians, who were licensed to meet in the house of Daniel Mansfield. They died out in the early 1800s. As we have seen, the Fringford rectors were very caring for their congregation in the nineteenth century. They were also used to controlling their parishioners and were not inclined to be tolerant of the few Nonconformists or 'dissenters' who lived in the village. In 1817, Roundell commented on 'two young men of loose and idle habits who frequent, I am told, a small meeting house in Hethe'![19] In 1838, there were 'a few families of Wesleyan Methodists, no place of public worship'. Similarly in 1854, 'Dissent: no place. A few meet in a cottage - 3 families'.[20] Surviving Methodist records indicate that these were probably the Claydon, Cowley and Harris families. In the 1840s, the Wesleyans obtained licences to meet in the house of William Walker and later in that of Mrs Tame (or Thame) and Mrs Harris. The 1841 census seems to show that there were Harris and Thame families living in three adjoining houses.

Strangely, the religious census on 31 March 1851 records an Independent (or Congregational) congregation of 63 at the evening service in Fringford, although there is no other record of Independents in the village. The census also seems to point to the building of an Independent chapel in 1844. This was a period of revival for the Independents and it led to the building of new chapels in places like Blackthorn (1841), Ambrosden (1846) and Launton (1850). However, it is extremely difficult to reconcile the building of a chapel in Fringford with the other evidence, since there was almost no nonconformity in the village. The census probably refers to the use of the above dwelling houses for the meeting of a few families.

It was during this period that William Ferguson, the Independent minister of Launton, preached widely in the area; often in the open air where he would draw crowds of some 250 to 300. He was an outspoken and contentious figure during his local ministry from 1839 until 1860. At that point his alleged clerical delinquency with a former family governess forced him to flee to America with her! He preached in Stratton Audley in 1839 and over the years may well have done the same in Fringford.[21] However, there seems to be no valid evidence for a regular Independent congregation or chapel in Fringford. Even in Hethe, which had a strong Methodist congregation, there was no Wesleyan chapel until the early 1850s.

Chapter 4

Schools and Education

In 1973, the old National School, and the Hethe and Stratton Audley schools, closed and all the children moved across the Green into the 'new school'. Although numbers dropped to about 30 in 1986, the school has grown steadily since then to an all-time high of nearly 120. In 1998, the 'new school' celebrated its 25th anniversary, which was marked by a splendid reunion and the production of a fine commemorative book covering the 25 years. This chapter concentrates on the 'old school' and earlier education in the village.

As early as 1768, Dr Addington and John Russell Greenhill started a small school, teaching the catechism, reading and writing, in a house provided by Dr Addington. He and the rector paid the fees of twelve of the poorest children in the parish to attend the school. The teachers at the school (a brother and sister) were brought into the parish by Dr Addington, who also provided a home for them. By 1808, the school was 'kept by an industrious woman, who teaches them to read the catechisms'.[22] Lord Sidmouth (Dr Addington's son) and the rector were still paying for eight children. By 1823, and probably earlier, there were Sunday schools for boys and girls. By 1834, there were three daily schools, with 20 boys and 16 girls between the ages of three and nine, supported by parents, Lord Sidmouth and the rector; also Sunday schools for boys and girls, supported by the rector. Other parishes do not seem to have been so well supported, as Henry Roundell comments in 1838 that 'six places have no daily or Sunday school'.[23]

In 1854, there were 35 children at daily schools in the rector's barn, between Bancroft and the Old Rectory, where James Wood now writes his music for

FRINGFORD

percussion. These children were mainly paid for by the rector, Henry de Salis. There was also an infant school for 20 and Sunday schools for 40 boys and girls.[24] The bell, which you can see on the gable-end of the Old Rectory, looks like an old school bell. The rector probably put it up to call the children to their lessons. There is no record of the type of education in the daily schools, although there was concern expressed about the early age that children left to work on the farms or at lacemaking. This was a common problem in agricultural villages, where young boys were often involved in heavy and monotonous labour such as stone-picking and topping and tailing turnips and young girls in lacemaking and sewing.

In 1866, de Salis built the National School, which we now call the 'old school', on land leased from Mr Harrison. There was quite a spate of school-building in the area in this period: Hethe 1852, Cottisford 1856, Bucknell 1861, Lower Heyford 1867, Hardwick 1870 and Newton Purcell 1873. This is quite late for National schools to be built compared with other areas of the country. Most of them were paid for by one or two individuals, so it is no surprise to find de Salis paying for Fringford school. The school opened in 1866 with places for 80 pupils, although the average attendance for 1871 was 71. A schoolmaster, Edwin Blackburn, was appointed for the first time and his wife was employed as the sewing mistress. The lessons described in Lark Rise included 'a scripture lesson every morning and needle work every afternoon for the girls'.[25] As these lessons could earn the school a grant, no doubt they were encouraged. The Old School House was built for them in 1876 on land leased from Lord Sidmouth. After the first schoolmaster, all the teachers were female until the arrival of William Robinson in 1910. He was a busy man, if perhaps not always a popular one, as he was also assistant overseer and the local assessor and collector of taxes.

Top: School children in front of the Old School c.1910 (Sue Gahan)

Middle left: School group in front of the Hut in the late 1930s, with the staff in the front row: Miss Hayes, Mrs Waring, Miss Harris (later Mrs Crook) and Mr Lanham, headteacher (Gladys Hinks)

Middle right: School staff in late 1940s: Mr and Mrs Standen and Mrs Wyatt (on right) (Judy Legg)

Bottom: The Old School in the 1950s before the building was joined to the hut. Note the railings put in the gap following the death of an evacuee (Judy Legg)

There was also some education for parents who were interested. De Salis started singing classes in the evening for them and in 1866 there were two evening classes. These seem to have been discontinued under Coker, although three of his daughters helped in the Sunday schools on a voluntary basis. Sunday schools continued under his successors and there were three or four voluntary teachers in 1899. There must also have been evening classes from time to time, because in 1911 the school managers were hoping that evening classes would be opened during the ensuing winter, which classes they thought were much needed in the parish.

In 1902, the local authorities were given responsibility for elementary and secondary education. Although the old School Board was abolished and the school managers formed a new Education Committee, the school continued to be church-aided. The leaving age was now twelve, except for children employed in agriculture. Numbers on roll continued to be about 60 and the minutes and logbooks do not indicate much in the way of change. There is continuing concern over 'the outside offices' (i.e. the toilets), culminating in complaints from the District Inspector of Nuisances in 1912! There was also some concern in 1910 when a teacher, Miss Blackshaw, announced her approaching marriage. Fortunately for her 'the Managers saw no reason to terminate her engagement on that account'! There were some serious epidemics in this period and two children died of diphtheria in 1913.

During the First World War there are very few references to the fighting in the logbook and the minutes. Gardening was added to the curriculum in 1914 and the subject was taken seriously with the need for extra food during wartime. The rector provided a plot in the Bridge Ground allotments near Fringford Bridge and in 1915 Arthur Jepson, the headmaster, passed the exam in Cottage and Allotment Gardening held by the Royal Horticultural Society. There were few other changes in the curriculum and attendance could still be erratic in such an agricultural community.

A late harvest, for example, could delay the start of school, as it did in September 1917 when the children were granted an additional week's holiday. The children were needed to help their mothers gleaning at the end of the harvest and the school managers had little hope of getting many children to school. The potato harvest in September and October could have a similar effect, particularly in wartime, and there were school holidays of a week or more for the harvest during both World

Wars. The children were also given a series of half-holidays to pick blackberries (to make jam) for the Army and Navy in 1917 and 1918. As a result, in July 1917 the Government had to announce that marks lost by children employed in harvests after the holidays would be allowed for. There is no mention of the Armistice in November 1918 but we do hear of the national holiday given for Peace Festivities on 18 July 1919. In 1918, the school leaving age was raised to fourteen.

In 1929, a fourth classroom was added, allowing the admission of older children from six other schools, Finmere, Hethe, Stratton Audley, Cottisford, Newton Purcell and Mixbury. This increased the roll from 50 to about 90. In 1932, Sarah Rennison commented, 'No one is having children now. There is not many in the place. They have to come from several villages all round to fill the school'![26] Bicester Grammar School had opened in 1924 but few children from Fringford School achieved entry to it. A fifth classroom (the present playgroup hut) was erected in 1931 at a cost of £125, mainly for practical work. This was not connected to the main building and there was an unfortunate accident early in the Second World War. One of the evacuees ran through the gap and was knocked down and killed by the lemonade lorry coming from 'Granny Wright's' shop. A steel railing was erected across the gap as a temporary safety measure. It was not until 1960 that a new store was built between the main school and the hut, thus eliminating the rather dangerous passage entrance from the school into Rectory Lane.

In 1939, soon after the outbreak of war, a few evacuees started arriving from London by private arrangement. In June 1940, a party of 40 evacuee children from the William McGuffie School in Walthamstow was formally admitted, accompanied by two teachers. This enlarged the school to five classes with 140 on roll. The numbers on roll were fairly steady after this, although there were 159 by October 1940. This must have been a major disruption to the life of the school and the local residents, who gave them homes. The logbook comments that the evacuees 'are constantly changing, some returning to their home towns and others being admitted, so that the classes are by no means settled'. The evacuee teachers also changed. There were still 50 evacuees in 1942 and even in 1944 there were 20. All except the last four returned in June 1945 and the numbers on roll were down to 90 by September. There are various mentions of the War but only two air-raid alerts - both on 28 February 1941. It was in the same year that a Blenheim bomber crashed on Juniper Hill, killing the pilot and little Edith Pratt.

An unusual headmaster's 'handover' letter from Harold Corfe to Jack Standen survives from June 1944. After 39 years in Tottenham and the headship of a large council school there, Corfe led an evacuation party of 400 from Tottenham to the Fen District in September 1939 and organised their settlement. In June 1940, he led another party of evacuees to South Wales, where he became acting head of a large mixed school of some 300 evacuee children. He was thus unusually well qualified to come to Fringford in 1942. He left at very short notice in May 1944, when his wife became seriously ill. A number of his comments about the school and the school house make amusing reading in our age of rather over-organised education:

'Managers won't interfere with you - tho'perhaps a Mr Cross - a youngish man from Finmere - might be inquisitive about Scripture'.
'Water : the pump in the scullery and the water from it not fit to poison pigs. All the drinking water in buckets from village pump - 50 yards.'
'Timetable - Nobody has bothered about a Timetable. I made out a complete one early on and it is somewhere in the desk in the 'Hut' (i.e. the playgroup building). *It serves as a timetable - used elastically. There are so many interruptions it is a practical impossibility to keep a timetable'.*
'The Admission Register is not "up to date". The Summary Register - I never made it up at all last year - a farce.'
'Sch. Milk Scheme: Mr Buckingham - across the Green - supplies (i.e. from Hall Farm). *Children bring milk across in morning. Two each week supervise distribution and clean bottles.'*
'P.S. I believe you will like Fringford - it should serve your purpose well - its lovely country - You'll want for nothing - and - in a few years there will be great developments just the other side of Bicester - with new schools wanting headmasters. Get "dug" in for a year or two & keep your eyes open.'[27]

This was very true, of course, about the future development of Bicester, but Jack Standen stayed on as Head until his retirement in 1963. He and his family had been evacuated from London to Wales. They moved to Fringford because their daughter Judy's education began to suffer with most of her lessons in Welsh. They had rented out their Wimbledon home and had planned to return there after the War. However, under the then current legislation, it was extremely difficult to evict sitting tenants. Jack appealed directly to Parliament and Winston Churchill used the 'Standen Case' to tackle the plight of evacuated families and amend the law relating to sitting tenants. Churchill's note of thanks to Jack has survived (see Appendix 3), to provide Fringford with a slender link with the Great Man. Eventually, Wimbledon Council were given permission to buy the Standens' house and this enabled them to build Bancroft for their retirement.

In 1946, the leaving age was raised to 15. Attendance could still be erratic. In October 1946, for example, when food shortages and strict rationing still prevailed, there were a large number of absentees for the potato harvest. In 1949, the school was reorganised as a Junior Central School, with ages 5-7 coming from Fringford and Godington, and ages 7-11 from Fringford, Mixbury, Hethe, Hardwick, Godington, Cotmore and Caversfield. There were now only three classes and the numbers dropped from about 90 to 69. Seniors moved on to Bicester, where the new Highfield Secondary Modern school was built off Queen's Avenue in 1952. In 1963, the Grammar School moved to the same site and in 1965, the two schools were amalgamated into Bicester School (subsequently Bicester Community College from September 1987). In 1951, owing to the increasing problems and costs of repairs and maintenance, the managers decided to hand the school over to the LEA and it became church-controlled rather than church-aided. Apart from the building of the canteen in 1952 and the new stores and 'offices' in 1960, the 'old school' remained much the same until 1973, when it was closed and the 'new school' was opened. The 'old school' became a Victorian Study Centre and in the early 1980s 'the Hut' became home for the playgroup. The Centre is now closed and there are plans to develop the whole site.

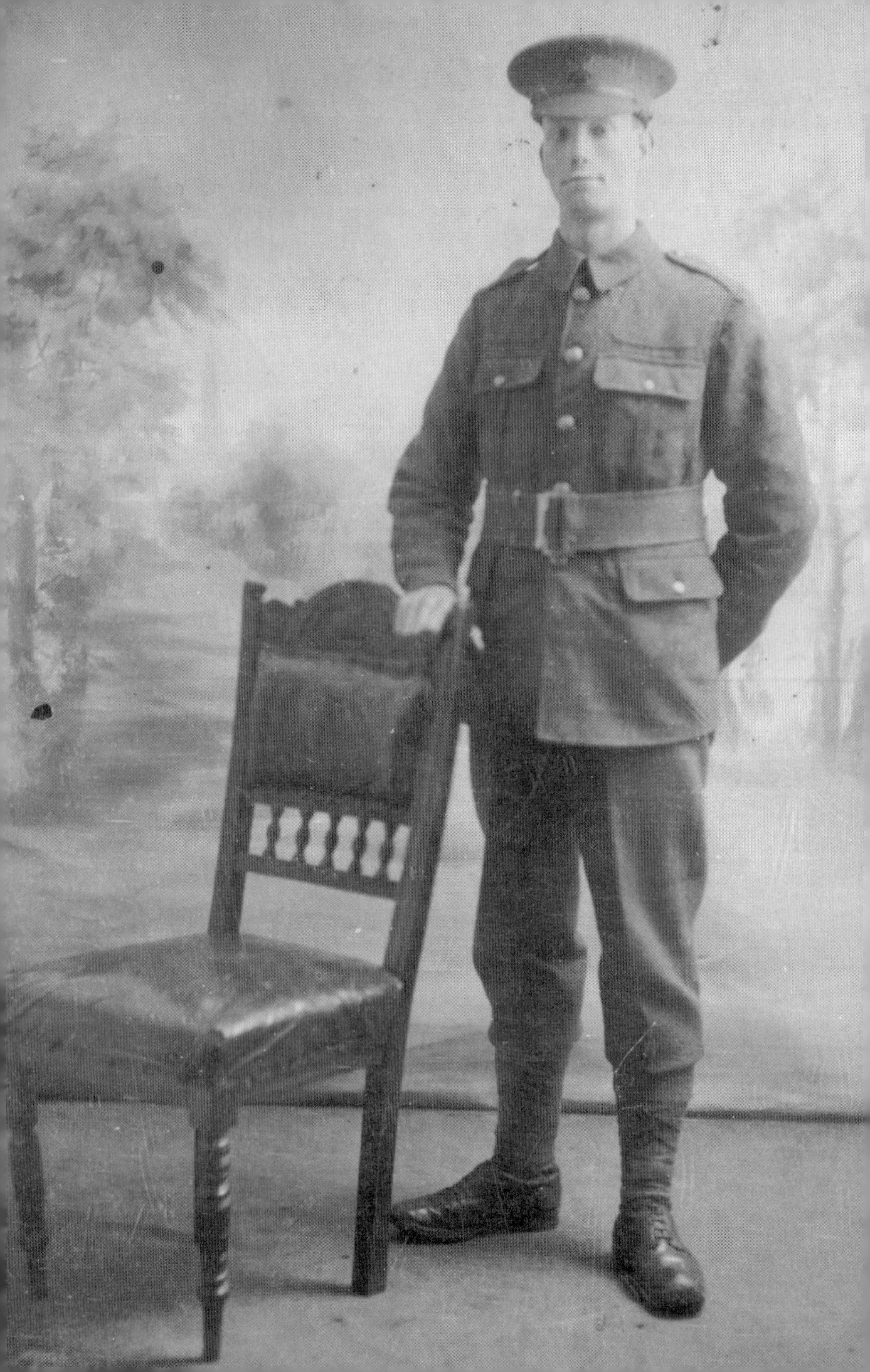

Chapter 5

The Roll of Honour

The names of five men from the village who died in the Great War, now known as the First World War, are recorded on the War Memorial in the churchyard. Research to date has revealed the following about them and those who gave their lives in the Second World War. Further research may reveal more about them and their families. I should be glad to receive any further personal details or photographs of them.

1914-1918

Frederick James Batchelor, son of Robert and Anne Batchelor of Green Farm, Fringford. Private 1st/18th Battalion, Royal Warks Regiment, died 27 August 1917, aged 28. Buried at Tyne Memorial Cemetery, Zonnebeke, Belgium.

John William Gerring, son of James and Jane Gerring of Main Street, Fringford. Private 84598 11th Company, Machine Gun Corps, died 22 December 1917, aged 23. Buried at Windmill B. Cemetery, Monchy le Preux, Pas de Calais.
    Jimmy Gerring was the church sexton for many years.

Charles Thomas Marriot, Private, Oxon and Bucks Regiment, aged 21.
 A Mrs Marriot was a sister of Jimmy Gerring, so Charles Marriot and John Gerring were probably cousins.

Charles Ernest Richardson, Private, Royal Warks Regiment, aged 21.
        A Mrs Richardson was Head of Fringford School about 1890-1900 and later lived in Folly Cottages. Charles may have been her son.

Jack Gerring, killed in action 1917 (Sue Gahan)

Alfred Waring, son of H.Waring and husband of Mrs A.W. Waring of Rectory Lodge, Tingewick, Bucks. Trooper 968, Royal Bucks Hussars, died 21 August 1915, aged 38. Buried at Helles Memorial, Gallipoli Peninsula, Turkey.

      A Mrs Waring was the Infants teacher at Fringford School between the Wars and she lived at Rose Cottage, Rectory Lane. Alfred could have been her husband's older brother.

Four other men who died in the Great War or the Boer War are commemorated in the church. Two of them were members of the Revd Coker's family. Their names are recorded on plaques below the second window in the north aisle, which was dedicated to the Cokers in 1898:

Cadwallader John Coker, younger son of James Gould and Florence Emily Coker, killed in action at St Eloi, 22 June 1915, aged 23. Laid to rest at Dickebush, Flanders.

Alexander Spearman R.N. Commander Collingwood Battalion, R.N.D. Husband of Jessie Aubrey Coker, daughter of Revd Cadwallader Coker. Killed in action in the Dardanelles, 4 June 1915.

The third man is commemorated in the first window in the north aisle. He was a member of the squire's family:

Edward John Dewar, Captain 60th Rifles, who died on 20 February 1900 of wounds received in action at Paardeburg, South Africa, while serving with the Mounted Infantry, aged 36.

The fourth man is commemorated on a plaque by the south door. I have no information on his family and connection with the village:

James Dixon, Captain and Adjutant 2nd Battalion Middlesex Regiment, born 6 May 1884. Fell in action Neuve Chapelle, 10 March 1915.

1939-1945

John Edward Blake (always known as Jack), son of Walter and Anne Blake and husband of Elsie Nellie Blake of Twyford, Bucks. Private 10592529 R.A.O.C., died 15 March 1945, aged 37. Buried at Schoonselhof Cemetery, Antwerp.

Gordon John Hancock, son of Hubert Gerald and Constance Annie Hancock of Eaton Socon, Bucks. Driver T/5383004,18 Supply Group, R.A.S.C., died 25 July 1943. Buried at Kanchanaburi Cemetery, Thailand (129 km NW of Bangkok).

Bert Hancock had lived at Green Farm, Fringford, when he was the village baker. His mother had been Head of Cottisford School.

We should also remember those who fought in the two Wars and lived to tell the tale. Some of them are still living in the village, like Les Golder, Bill Grantham, Jack Hodges and George Stathers. Jack's father went right through the Great War unscathed and also did home duties throughout the Second World War.

Leslie Morgan, former village baker at The Old Bakehouse, is no longer living but deserves a special mention. He served in 115 Squadron in the RAF as an air gunner and wireless operator. The squadron was equipped with Lancaster bombers and due to the type of targets allocated to it, Les's had the highest casualty rate of any on Bomber Command. Les's logbook, which his son Clive has kept, shows that he flew 38 missions over Germany, including several of the massive bomber raids. He was awarded the Belgian Croix de Guerre with palm for his contribution to the liberation of Belgium. He was also involved in rescuing other members of the crew when his plane crashed in flames. He flew transport missions in India after the German raids. In the village he never spoke of his wartime experiences and he was more famous for the quality of his cakes. He and his wife ran the Stratton Audley post office after he gave up the bakery.

Les Morgan (on the right) with an RAF friend (Clive Morgan)

If we look back further to the Boer War (1899-1902), at least two village families were represented. William Grantham, Bill's father, was a private in the Prince of Wales's Own, and he received a fine engraved clock and barometer from the village on his return from the war. Fred White also served in the war and received the same gifts from the village. The South African War, as it was generally called at the time, aroused huge emotions in England, particularly after the Relief of Mafeking, which was defended by Baden-Powell for 217 days. The Relief was widely celebrated in most towns and villages and there was a special public holiday on 25 May 1900. The return of the soldiers would have been an emotional moment and these special gifts to William and Fred from the village would have been a natural response.

Chapter 6

Candleford Green Revisited

'Candleford Green was taking its afternoon nap when they arrived. The large irregular square of turf which gave the village its name was deserted but for one grazing donkey and a flock of geese which came cackling with outstretched necks towards the spring-cart to investigate. ...The children who at other times played there were in school and their fathers were at work in the fields, or in workshops, or at their different jobs in Candleford town.'

'On the farther, less populated side of the green a white horse stood under a tree outside the smithy waiting its turn to be shod, and, from within, as the spring-cart drew up, the ring of the anvil and the roar of the bellows could be heard'.[28]

This was the scene in 1891 when the fourteen-year-old Laura (Flora Timms) arrived in Candleford Green to work at the sub-post office. Some 60 years later, after the Second World War, the scene would have been very similar. 'Noah' Price's pony might have been grazing on the Green and the children were still going to the Old School. There was little change round the Green after the village hall was built in 1900, until the council houses were built there in the 1950s and the new school in 1972. As in 1891, many of the men would have been working in the fields, on the Shelswell Estate or in their workshops. Others had found jobs outside the village, for example at the Heyford Air Base, the Bicester Ordnance Depot or the Calvert Brick Works. Outside the old forge a horse and some farm machinery would probably have been waiting for the attention of Ernie Perrin. There might also have

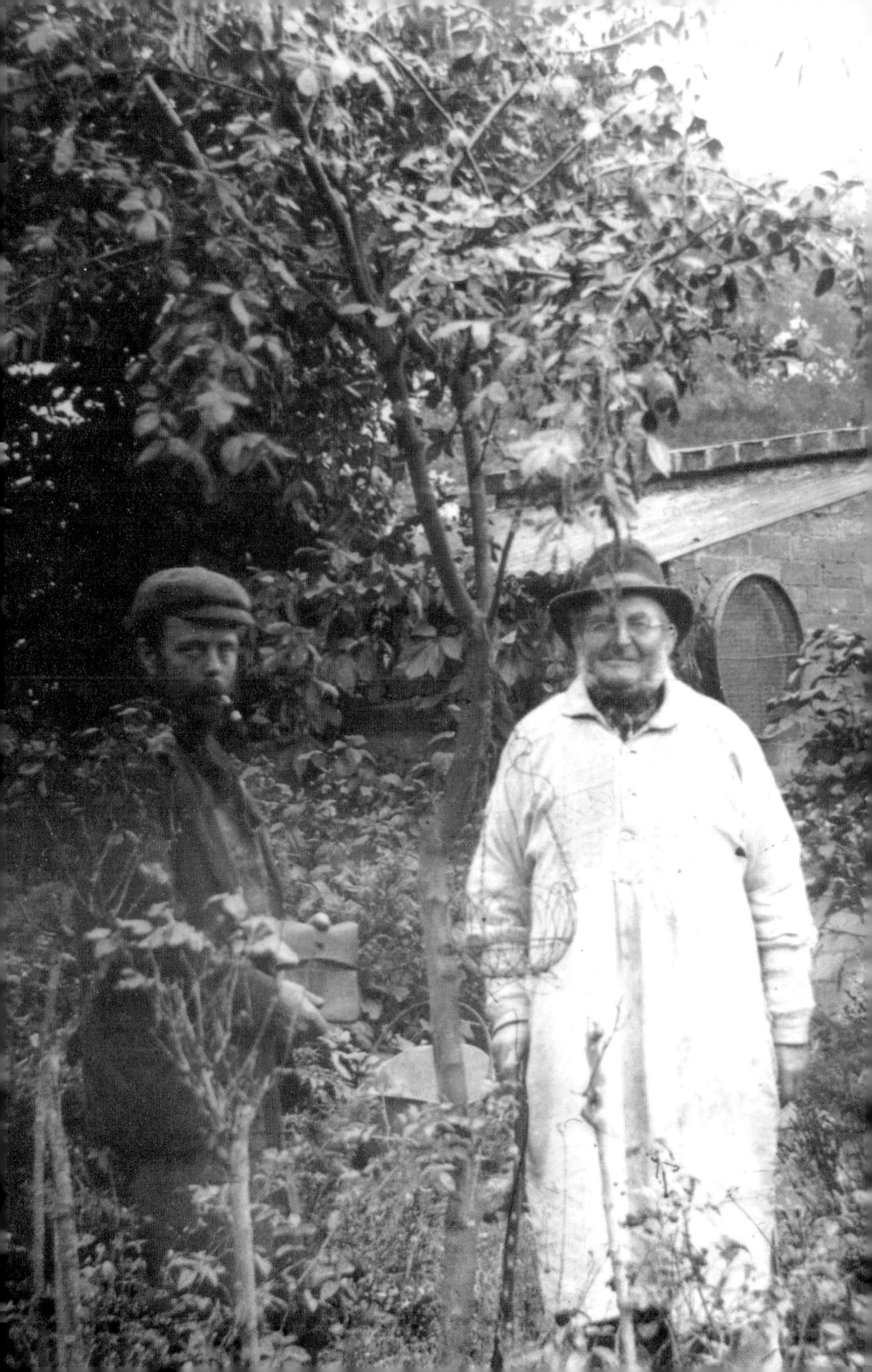

been a car or two awaiting William Plumb's magic touch. In his spare time from the Morris Works, he would repair cars and other engines, including his old Bullnose Morris (bought from William Grantham for 30 shillings!).

'Mrs Gubbins had got herself up to face the weather by tying a red knitted shawl over her head and wearing the bottom of a man's trouser-legs as gaiters'.[29]

Late in 1891, Laura was overjoyed when she was allowed to start delivering letters rather than just sorting them in the office. She joined Mrs Gubbins, an older lady, in doing the cross-country deliveries and her round included Willaston, Shelswell and the estate cottages. By a happy coincidence, we know something of a later Fringford letter-carrier, Sarah Butler, who was born in Fringford in 1850 and married William Rennison. She is recorded as a dressmaker in the 1891 census, living with her son and a blind lodger, Charles Thame, who may have been a cousin. A letter, written to her brother during the First World War, shows that she must have been doing almost exactly the same morning round as Laura and wrapping up like Mrs Gubbins to keep out the cold. 'They told me this morning that I looked like a red Indian in my big boots and gaiters and waterproof skirt and my red face'.[30] By then she was well over sixty, living in one end of Church Farm and working for Ernest and Elsie Price, who had been running the post office since about 1910. She comments that it was hard work at her age and she had to reserve her strength to carry the letters and parcels. Otherwise she would have joined the women and children catching crabs (i.e.crayfish); this would have been in the brook down by the mill. In wartime they could get '1s per bushel for the government to use the acid in making shells at Birmingham'. Her photograph, taken behind Church Farm sometime in the 1920s, shows a very strong and determined lady. We do not know how long she continued to do the letter round but she lived on in Fringford on her own until 1932. Only then, aged 82, did she reluctantly agree to join her son near Bristol and she died there in the following year.

Village life in Sarah Rennison's time had clearly changed little from the time of Flora Thompson. The life recalled by older residents from their youth also has more echoes of Candleford Green than it does of life at the end of the twentieth century. Daily life was simple with few luxuries. The community remained close-knit and mainly self-sufficient, with its own shops, craftsmen and tradesmen. The population in 1951 was much the same as it had been in 1901 (about 340) and most families

William Plumb (in smock) with Thomas Deeley in the garden of the Old Forge. Note the privy in the background (Bill Plumb)

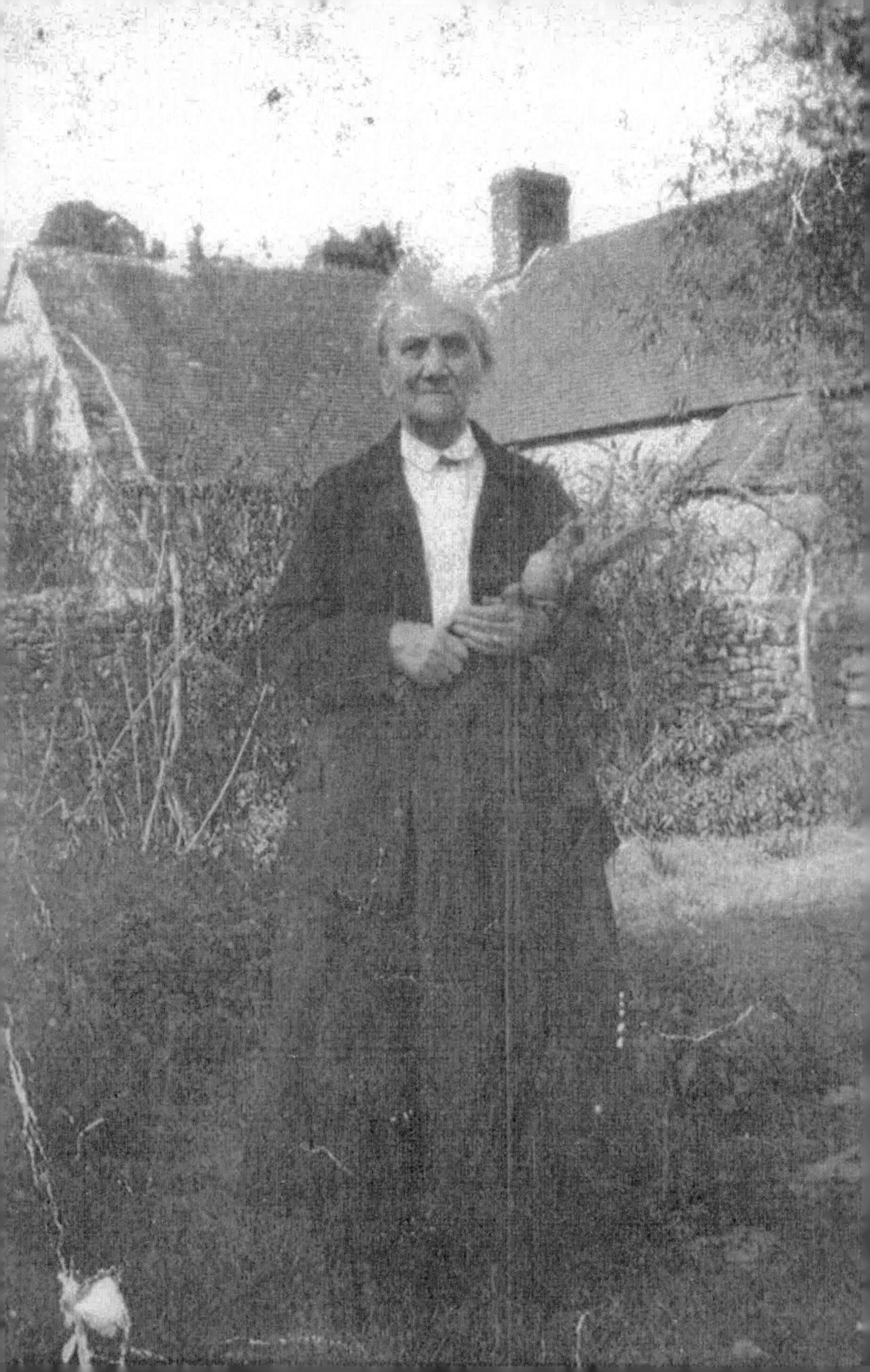

remained largely dependent on agriculture. Electricity was not in general use until after the Second World War and most families were still using water from wells or the village pumps. When the council houses were built on the Stratton Audley Road in the early 1950s, a water tower had to be built just beyond the pub to supply them. These houses had all the modern conveniences but the standard of the older houses was still very basic and many of them were in a very poor state of repair. New housing developments and barn conversions were still many years ahead.

The BBC had started broadcasting in 1922 and most people bought wirelesses. In the absence of electricity in the homes, these were run off accumulators. Children used to take these over to Tommy Allen's shop in Hethe or to Billy Judd in Rectory Lane to be re-charged. Television did not make its appearance until the 1950s and it was a long time before it was generally affordable. The telephone was not in general use until after the Second World War. The Kelly's Directory of 1939 is the first one to mention telephone numbers in the village. It records Cecil Cross, the butcher, as Stratton Audley 23 and Ernest Price at the post office as 20 - a far cry from today's six-figure numbers. Most people had to use the telephone kiosk outside the post office. At this stage there was no direct dialling and all numbers had to be obtained through the local exchange at Stratton Audley.

Village shops

In the early 1950s memories of the Second World War were still fresh in people's minds. The period of austerity continued, with rationing for food, clothing, petrol and many domestic commodities surviving until 1954. In 1941, the weekly meat ration had been as little as half a pound per person, about a shilling's worth (5p), which in a comfortable pre-war household would have constituted a single helping! Weekly rations of other basic foods were similarly meagre: 1oz cheese, 4oz bacon or ham, 8oz sugar, 8oz fats (including not more than 2oz butter) and 2oz jam or marmalade. There were some extra rations for agricultural workers and miners. This may have been a period of austerity but it was not all gloom, as some historians would have you believe. Many people had been used to 'getting by' even before the War and there was great relief at the arrival of peace. For children, there was also great excitement, when it was possible to buy your first bar of chocolate and your first ice-cream. Other treats were the first bananas and fresh eggs after all the

Sarah Rennison behind Church Farm in the 1920s (Elizabeth Bagley)

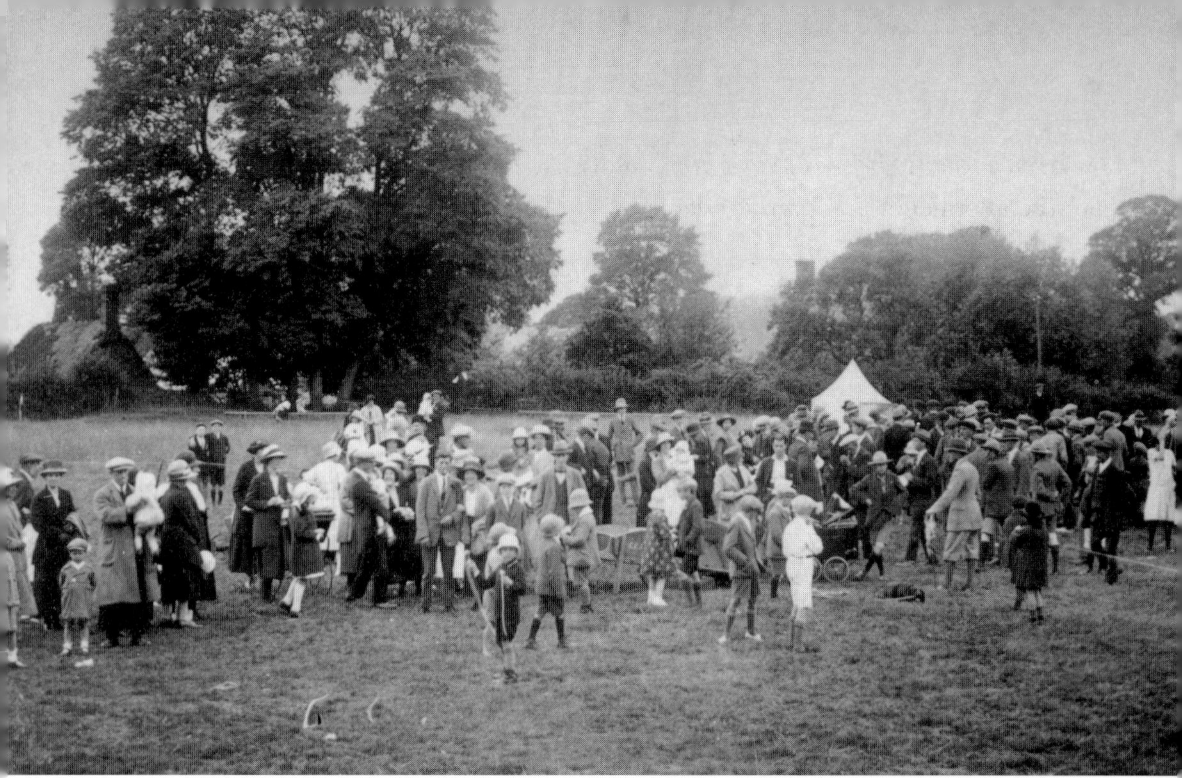
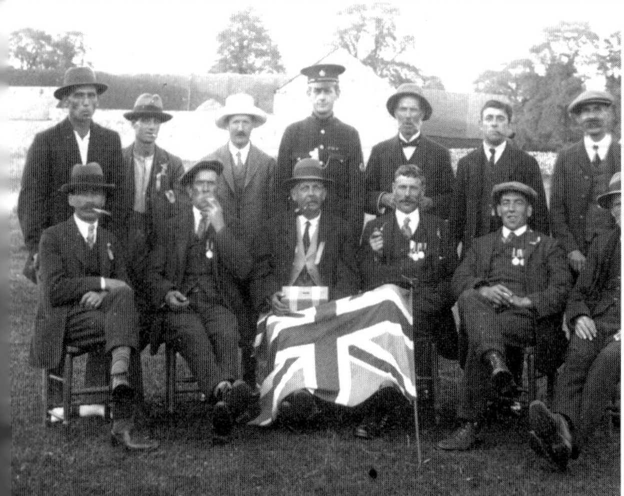
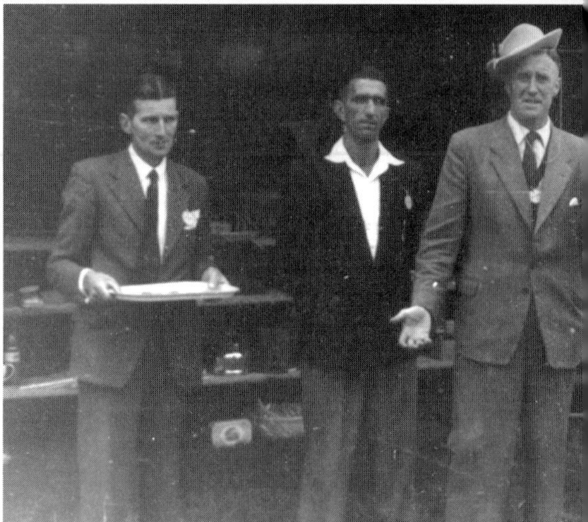
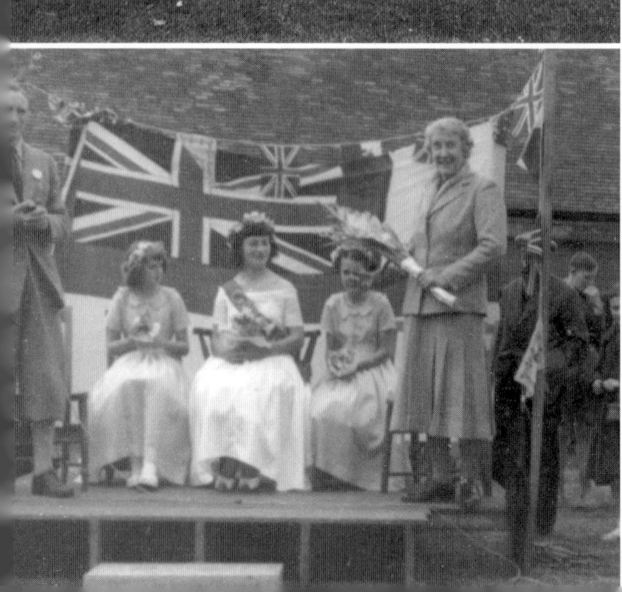
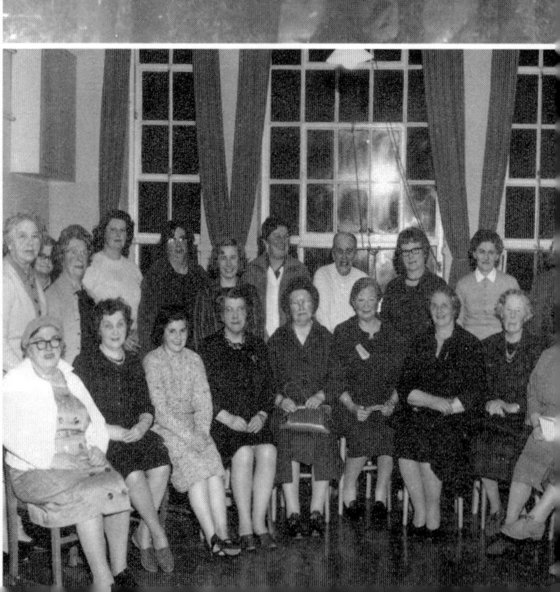

powdered egg, although, in a rural community like Fringford, fresh eggs and produce from the allotments had been available.

So, if you were out to do your morning shopping in the early 1950s, there was some opportunity to buy more than the basic necessities. There was also the chance to catch up on all the local gossip, at a time when you probably knew almost everyone in the village. Your first stop might have been at 'Old Lizzie's' (Stone Gap Cottage), where Lizzie Grantham had been selling sweets, tobacco and cigarettes since the early 1930s. Phil Green had helped then to fit out the shop. Here you could buy a halfpenny bag of sweets for the children. Across the road you would have bought your small weekly meat ration from Cecil Cross (Rosecroft). Then, if you wanted a postal order, you would have carried on towards the Manor. 'Down the muddy track', said a child in 1972 pointing a stubby finger towards the farmyard, 'along by the wall and you'll see a gate. Go in there, past the runner beans and the carrots and that's where it is.'[31] Here, at no.6, you would have found Laura Powell in one of the smallest post offices in England. She had taken over the duties in 1949, when Ernest and Elsie Price gave up the post office on Rectory Lane. She was to continue running it until 1986 and by then it was the only shop left in the village.

On your return journey, you might have seen the Manor cows waiting to be milked in the yard by the West Barns. In those days, the Manor had its own milking parlour and a horse pulled a turntable to provide power for it. You might have called in at Mansfield Yard to get some supplies from Emily Hinks's shop and to pick up your watch from William Elderfield. Here you would have enjoyed the array of striking

Top: Club Day on the Green in the 1920s; Ellis Chinnery in plus-fours (Gordon Allen)

Middle left: Club Committee in the 1920s. Front row from right to left: Bill Wright, unknown, Bert White, Happy Hinks, Mark Hutton, Harry Batchelor. Back row: George Mansfield, Arthur Cawston, 2 unknowns, Ernie Watts (Waterloo Farm), Twink Hutton, Bill Golder (Gordon Allen)

Middle right: Jack Wise, Tom Bartlett and Arthur James - the Sports Club Carnival Committee in the early 1950s (Judy Legg)

Bottom left: Beauty Queen 1953, Rosemary Smith with Wendy James (left) and Ann Lloyd. Mrs Chinnery is holding the flowers (Judy Legg)

Bottom right: Womens Institute group in the 1950s. Miss Tomkinson is fourth from the right in the front row. This row also includes Mrs Standen and her two sisters, the Misses Preedy, who came to live in Pringle Cottage (Judy Legg)

Lizzie Grantham in front of her shop - Stone Gap Cottage (Bill Grantham)

clocks and watches in his workshop, if he was not away in Oxford making his twice-weekly deliveries and collections. The next call on your way back to the Green might have been at Church Farm to pick up some milk from Frank Sumner, although he was still delivering daily, carrying two milk churns on a yoke across his shoulders.

If you lived on Rectory Lane, you would probably have done some of your shopping at 'Mrs Carey's' grocery shop and 'Granny Wright's' sweet shop in Prentice Yard. Mrs Carey died just before the war but Miss Hutton and then the Savins ran the shop, until the row of cottages was demolished in the early 1950s. Miss Hitchhcock also had a small sweet shop on Rectory Lane. After all these shops had closed, you would have done your grocery shopping at Mrs Omar's by the cricket ground, until it, too, closed down in the late 1970s. You would have continued to buy your bread at the Old Bakehouse, until Les Morgan retired in the late 1960s. These village shops would not have met all your needs. Once a week you would have walked out to the main road to catch one of the regular buses to Bicester, to enjoy a wider choice in the larger shops. On your return journey you would have earned yourself a drink at the Butchers Arms, where Albert Green, Phil's father, had been presiding since 1913! He was not to retire until 1955.

The millennium

A hundred years on from Laura's arrival in Candleford Green, we should be eternally grateful that Flora Thompson left such a vivid record of village life in Oxfordshire in the late nineteenth century. Her portrait of Candleford Green tells us so much about life in Fringford, as she looked back on it from the 1940s, and it provides a perfect starting point for a re-visit. As we move into the third millennium, there is still much in the village to interest her fans and much that she would still recognise, in spite of all the changes. The population has nearly doubled since 1951 to about 600 and most of the green spaces have been filled in. The old forge is silent, much farmland is 'set aside' and all the village shops are closed. In many families, both parents are now working and commuting away from the village. It is easier for them to do the shopping weekly at the supermarket and much more difficult for any village to support a shop.

It is tempting to look back to a golden age when there was more green and less noise. The era before the First World War has often been recalled as such a golden age, with idyllic childhoods and endless hot summers. Research has shown that such statements by contemporaries were all made after 1914![32] Many of the working class in that era were below the 'poverty line' and the 'long hot summer' of 1911, for example, was a period of major dock and rail strikes and the Liverpool riots. Similarly, the period between the Wars was for many people one of poverty and hardship. It is only in the last forty years that we have seen a huge rise in the general level of prosperity and the elimination of most poverty.

Today, there may not be the range of craftsmen and tradesmen that there were in Flora's day but the new generation of inhabitants possesses a great variety of skills. There are farmers, teachers, lawyers, surveyors, doctors, nurses, businessmen and businesswomen, builders, carpenters, and all manner of computer experts. The village may not be as closely-knit or self-supporting, but the range of activities which the village supports seems to be expanding. The Cricket Club continues to flourish and will celebrate its centenary next year, the School numbers are at an all-time high, the Playgroup flourishes and the Village Hall is the venue for a great variety of activities and entertainment. Candleford Fair is held every summer and this year, after many years, the ancient tradition of dancing round the maypole on May Day was revived. As is the case nationally, the church cannot be said to be flourishing but it is still in regular use and there are great plans for its restoration. The Shelswell Group is also exploring ways of using the ten churches more imaginatively in an effort to revive church attendance.

An ever-expanding Bicester poses a threat to all the surrounding villages. We must hope that Fringford will retain its separate identity and not be absorbed into the urban sprawl. In many respects, the village is now flourishing as never before and it seems possible to look forward to a positive future at the dawn of the third millennium.

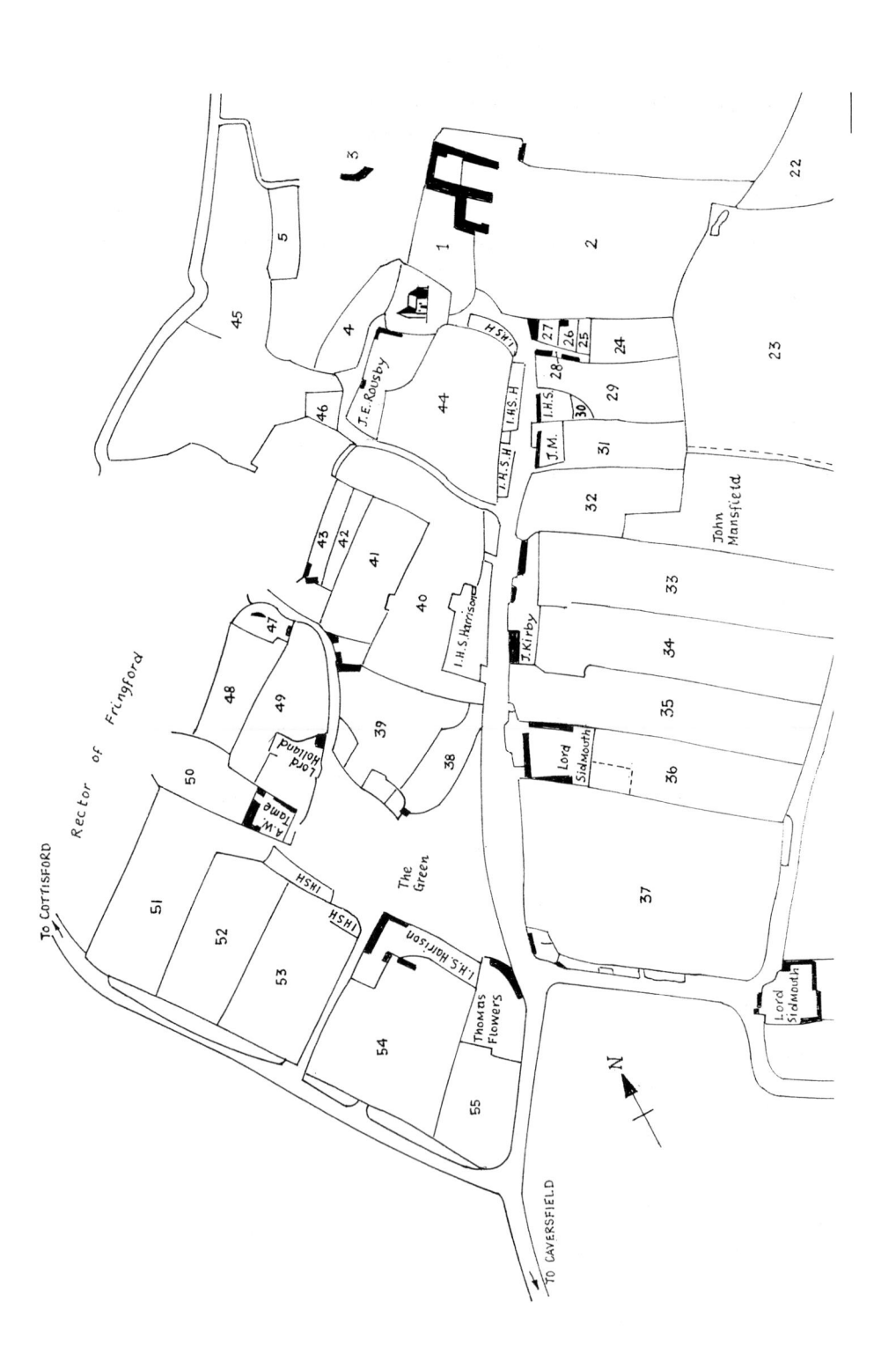

Tithe map of 1856

APPENDIX 1

Fringford Tithe Award with part of the Tithe Map of 1856
(references are to the 1856 map)

Ref. No.	Landowner	Occupier	Name of property
1	JH Slater-Harrison	Thos. Simons	Homestead orchard garden
2	do	do	Home close
3	do	do	Dairy ground
4	do	do	Garden
5	do	JHS-H	Plantation
6	do	Thos. Simons	Little meadow
7	do	do	Ozier bed meadow
8	do	do	Ozier bed
9	do	do	Newton meadow
10	JE Rousby(Eton Coll)	GS Waters	Mill holm
11	do	do	Mill leys
12	JHS-H	Thos. Simons	Lower heath
13	do	Himself	Middle heath
14	do	Thos. Simons	Upper heath
15	James Grantham	Himself	Home close
16	Viscount Sidmouth	GS Waters	New close
17	do	John Mansfield	New close
18	Thos. Flowers	Thos. Bailiss	New close
19	JHS-H	Thos. Simons	Diggins
20	do	do	Swains meadow
21	do	do	Pendalls ground
22	do	do	Ashills meadow
23	do	do	Ryehill meadow inc.Freeboard
24	William Mansfield	Himself	Garden
25	George Mansfield	Himself	Garden
26	David Mansfield	Himself	House & garden
27	Wm Mansfield	Himself	House & garden
28	George Mansfield	Himself	House outbuildings & yard
29	JHS-H	Thos. Simons	Beaufoots close
30	John Cotterell	Himself	Garden
31	John Mansfield	Himself	Waters close
32	JHS-H	Thos. Simons	May's close
33	Thos. Flowers	Thos. Bailiss	Smiths close
34	Viscount Sidmouth	John Mansfield	Walnut tree close
35	JHS-H	Thos. Simons	Ladymans close
36	Viscount Sidmouth	John Mansfield	Home close
37	JHS-H	Thos. Simons	Peakes close
38	do	do	Bulls close
39	Viscount Sidmouth	John Mansfield	School House close
40	JHS-H	Thos. Simons	Barretts close
41	Viscount Sidmouth	John Mansfield	Saul's close
42	Revd HD Roundell	Himself	Gibbs close
43	do	do	Douglas close
44	JE Rousby (Eton Coll)	GS Waters	Home close

45	JE Rousby (Eton Coll)	GS Waters	Meadows
46	do	do	Orchard
47	Revd HD Roundell	Thos. Wrighton	Homestead & garden
48	do	do	Close
49	JHS-H	Thos. Simons	Cotts close
50	William Tame	George Mansfield	Wesears close
51	JHS-H	Thos. Simons	Spaceys or Knibbs close
52	William Tame	George Mansfield	Home close
53	JHS-H	Thos Simons	Home close
54	do	do	Twenty lands
55	Thos. Flowers	Thos. Bailiss	Home close
56	JE Rousby (Eton Coll)	GS Waters	Twenty lands
57	JHS-H	Thos. Simons	Pit piece
58	do	do	Upper Mangton or the Butts
59	do	do	Lower Mangton
60	do	do	Crabtree Piece
61	do	do	do
62	Thos. Flowers	Thos. Bailiss	Part of Pinhill close
63	JHS-H	John King	Pinhill close
64	Viscount Sidmouth	John Mansfield	Hedgeway
65	JHS-H	John King	Colehill meadow
66	do	do	Colehill
67	do	do	Middle ground
68	do	do	Hedgeway
69	Viscount Sidmouth	John Mansfield	Waddington's close
70	JHS-H	John King	do
71	do	do	Lords mead
72	do	do	Stretchill ground
73	Viscount Sidmouth	John Mansfield	Beggars bridge
74	JHS-H	John King	Barn ground
75	do	do	Stone pit ground
76	do	do	Bainton ground
77	do	do	Home close
78	do	do	Homestead, garden & orchard
79	do	do	First furze ground
80	do	do	Meadow
81	do	Himself	Cotmoor Wood
82	do	do	Lower furze
83	do	do	Upper furze

Notes:
1. Under the Tithe Award, tithes (a tenth part of a person's income paid to the rector in cash or kind) were commuted to a rent-charge.
2. J.H.Slater-Harrison (JHS-H) owned 50 of the properties, of which Thomas Simons occupied 30.
3. Parcels 10, 11, 44, 45, 46, and 56 were the property of Eton College whose leaseholder was James Edward Rousby. The occupier of all the parcels was George Stimson Waters, who was probably the victualler at the Bricklayers Arms (now the Butchers Arms).
4. Parcels 10 and 11 covered Fringford Mill and parcels 44-46 Church Farm.
5. Parcels 56-73 covered the fields on either side of the Caversfield Road down to the crossroads.
6. Parcels 74-83 covered Cotmore, Moat Farm and the area beyond the crossroads.

APPENDIX 2
Fringford Rectors 1103-2000

1103	Earliest evidence of a church at Fringford. No evidence of a rector.
c.1215	Robert Picher
1233	Robert Lovel
1480-1523	Thomas Kirby
1565-1604	Richard Aldrich
1604-34	Emmanuel Scott
1634-45	William Overton (deposed)
1645-48	John Bayley (deposed by Cromwell)
1660-97	John Bayley (returned under Charles II)
1697	Matthew Tanjoux (died same year)
1697-1726	Bernard Gilpin
1726-41	Joseph Barnes
1735-56	Daniel Wardle. Curate in charge 1741-53, Rector 1753-56
1756-1813	John Russell Greenhill
1814-52	Henry D. Roundell
1852-73	Henry J. de Salis
1873-94	Cadwallader Coker
1894-98	Charles S. Thompson
1898-1910	R. Douglas Clarke
1910-21	Stafford Meredith Brown
1921-24	Archdeacon Whylock Pendavis. Rector of Fringford and Hethe from 1924.
1925-31	Leslie Brasnett
1931-48	John Harrington
1948-53	Horace Jones
1954-63	John Westlake. Rector of Newton Purcell with Fringford & Hethe.
1964-67	David I. Fraser
1968-78	John M. Sergeant
1978-95	Anthony Hichens (from 1983 Rector of the five Southern parishes).
1995-	Ricky Yates (Rector of the ten parishes in the Shelswell Group)

APPENDIX 3

Note from Winston Churchill to Jack Standen in 1945

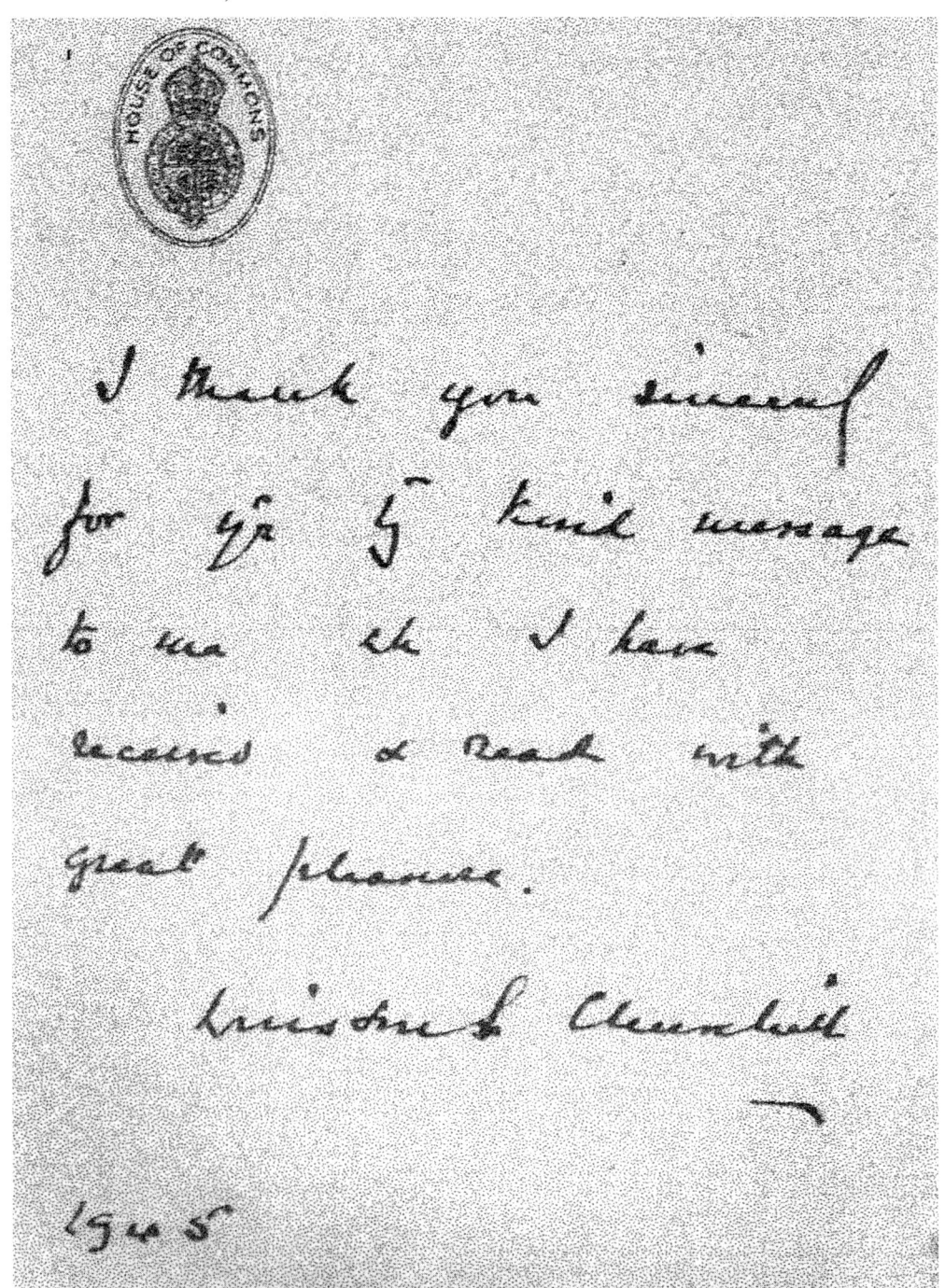

> I thank you sincerely for yr kind message to me wh I have received & read with great pleasure.
>
> Winston S. Churchill
>
> 1945

Churchill's note of thanks to Jack Standen for bringing to his attention the problem of evicting tenants from the Standens' home in Wimbledon. Churchill used the 'Standen Case' to amend the law relating to sitting tenants.

BIBLIOGRAPHY

I attach a list of the main primary and published sources, which I have consulted, for those who may wish to explore the history of the village further. I have tried to limit the number of detailed references below, because in many cases the source of the information will be obvious to those interested. Abbreviations, where necessary, are in brackets.

Primary Sources

Census records 1801-91
Churchwardens' accounts
Directories, including: *Gardner's, Kelly's, Post Office.*
The Revd John Russell Greenhill   *Diaries 1780-87* and *1793-1800*
M.W.Greenwood   *Parishes, Parsons and Persuasions: The contrasting clerics and communities of Fringford and Fritwell in 19th-century North Oxfordshire* (1997)
OAU Occasional Paper No. 6: *Excavations at The Paddock Rectory Lane Fringford* (February 2000) (OAU Paper No.6, 2000)
Oxford Diocesan records (MS. Oxf. Dioc.)
Parish registers
School logbooks 1910-90
School minutes 1904-65

Published Sources

E.M.G. Belfield	*The Annals of the Addington Family* (1959)
J.C. Blomfield	*History of the Deanery of Bicester, Part V* (1890/91) (Blomfield *Fringford*)
Christine Bloxham	*The World of Flora Thompson* (1998)
The Friends of Fringford School	*Fringford Church of England Primary School. 25th Anniversary Yearbook 1972-1998* (1998)
Sid Hedges	*Bicester Wuz a Little Town* (1968)
Gillian Lindsay	*Flora Thompson: The Story of the 'Lark Rise' Writer* (1990)
The Rotary Club of Bicester	*The Bicester Story* (1999)
Flora Thompson	*Lark Rise to Candleford* (Penguin 1973) (*Lark Rise*)
John M. Sergeant	*A History of Fringford and Newton Purcell-cum-Shelswell* (1977)

The Victoria County History of Oxford, vi, *Ploughley Hundred* (1959)

DETAILED REFERENCES

[1] OAU Paper No. 6, 2000.
[2] Blomfield *Fringford*, 8-9.
[3] *Oxford Chronicle*, 16 Nov.1844.
[4] *Lark Rise*, 417.
[5] *Oxford Chronicle*, 16 Nov.1844.
[6] Jose Harris, *Private Lives, Public Spirit: Britain 1870-1914* (1993).
[7] Blomfield *Fringford*, 25.
[8] *Bicester Advertiser*, 4 Jan.1901.
[9] *Lark Rise*, 524.
[10] Letter from Tony & Mary Yoward to Mrs E.M.B. Young, 23 Sept. 1987.
[11] MS. Oxf. Dioc. b 70.
[12] Letter from H.A.Corfe to J.A.Standen, 11 June 1944.
[13] Blomfield *Fringford*, 38-9.
[14] MS. Oxf. Dioc. c 273.
[15] MS. Oxf. Dioc. d 550.
[16] MS. Oxf. Dioc. d 178.
[17] *Lark Rise*, 523-4.
[18] *Lark Rise*, 527.
[19] MS. Oxf. Dioc. d 576.
[20] MS. Oxf. Dioc. d 701.
[21] Largely based on unpublished notes of Pat Tucker of Launton.
[22] MS. Oxf. Dioc. d 707.
[23] MS. Oxf. Dioc. b 41.
[24] MS. Oxf. Dioc. b 70.
[25] *Lark Rise*, 178.
[26] Letter from Sarah Rennison to the Butler family, 25 July 1932.
[27] Letter from H.A.Corfe to J.A.Standen, 11 June 1944.
[28] *Lark Rise*, 393.
[29] *Lark Rise*, 504.
[30] Letter from Sarah Butler Rennison to her brother, Thomas Butler, undated (probably 1915-16).
[31] *Oxford Times*, 8 Sept. 1972.
[32] Barbara W. Tuchman, *The Proud Tower*, Foreword (1966).

CONTACT DETAILS

If you have further information on the people or places mentioned, or indeed on any aspect of this publication, please contact me on

+44 (0) 1869 278317,

or by e-mail to martin@mwgreenwood.fsnet.co.uk

Notes

Notes